HIDDEN
MANCHESTER

HIDDEN
MANCHESTER

by Glynis Cooper

breedon **books**
PUBLISHING

First published in Great Britain in 2004 by
The Breedon Books Publishing Company Limited
Breedon House, 3 The Parker Centre,
Derby, DE21 4SZ.

Dedicated to Liz,
a modern daughter of Manchester,
who had no idea what lay hidden
behind the façade.

ISBN 1 85983 401 9

Printed and bound by Butler & Tanner,
Frome, Somerset, England.

Cover printing by Lawrence-Allen Colour Printers,
Weston-super-Mare, Somerset, England.

Contents

Acknowledgements

The writer of this book is deeply indebted to the following:

Staff of the Archives and Local Studies department at Manchester Central Library, especially Paula Moorhouse and Margaret de Motte, for their unfailing help and patience.

Nigel Rudyard and Sue Doyle from 'Spinning the Web' (website writers and researchers based at Central Library) for their local knowledge and anecdotes.

Staff at all the institutions and organisations visited for research purposes, but particularly those at Chetham's Library, Manchester Cathedral Coffee Shop, the Jewish Museum, Taylor Woodrow, Mr Thomas's Chop House, Platt Hall, Quarry Bank Mill, and the Monastery Trust of St Francis and Gorton.

My daughter, Liz Reeve, for technical help.

My editor, Susan Last, and her staff for turning my jottings and photographs into a published work.

My long-suffering family who encouraged me in my writing and research, read drafts, cooked meals, made endless brews, ran errands, and wholeheartedly supported me.

Introduction

Cotton is that creative, vivifying, radiating power from which emanate the suns and stars and comets, the life and light and being of Manchester...

(Wheeler's *Manchester Chronicle*, 5 October 1833)

You hear nothing but the breathing of the vast machines sending forth fire and smoke through their tall chimneys...

(Leon Faucher, Manchester in 1844)

...the setting of the picture is ugly and grim enough. A black, mean looking street, with a black unadorned mill rising over the houses, and a black chimney pouring out smoke upon all...

(*Manchester and the Textile Districts in 1849*, Angus Bethune Reach, 1849)

The Age of Ruins is past. Have you seen Manchester? Manchester is as great a human exploit as Athens.

(Benjamin Disraeli in his novel *Coningsby*, published *c.*1887)

...Manchester seemed like the Garden of Eden...

(Jewish refugee in World War Two 1939–1945)

this isn't Paris...THIS is Manchester!

(promotional poster for Commonwealth Games, 2002)

MANCHESTER, it seems, can mean different things to different people, but the city has generally been perceived for too long as a grim, wet mucky place ('where there's muck there's brass' is an old northern saying), the workshop of the world, and hell if one lives there. But that is changing. Manchester is re-inventing itself. It is the second city of England; a vibrant exciting place where things are happening; and the city proudly proclaims this is not Venice... Vienna... New York... this is Manchester.

It is probably a peculiarity of the English language that one word can have so many different meanings. 'Hidden' would appear to have almost as much individual significance as the number of people who use it. To say that reaction to a book on 'Hidden Manchester' has been varied would be an understatement.

'Oh, what's hidden? Is it a sort of treasure?'

'I love history. You know, what's hidden below the surface.'

'Far too little written about the ghosts of Manchester.'

'Not another book about 'hidden' underground culture?'

'Will *Hidden Manchester* expose the real city?'

'What? The hidden activities of drug dealers and the black market?'

'Hidden? You mean not visible?'

'Good title for a book on archaeology. *Hidden Manchester.*'

'You mean things they don't want you to know about?'

'Hidden. Is that the sinister side of Manchester?'

'Things can remain hidden away for years. An exposé would be a good thing.'

'If it's hidden, is it fair to write about it because then everyone will know?'

Such a wide remit would give any writer nightmares since their readers seem to expect so many different things. As individual interpretation seems to be the order of the day, this writer decided that *Hidden Manchester* would mean 'unusual, perhaps not generally known, sometimes out of sight, more than a touch of the historical aspect plus a few unexplained tales and occasionally the mad or the bad, with the emphasis on readers being able to visit places for themselves to see what is there or to imagine what was there'.

So there are stories of lost rivers and canals; of graveyards hidden beneath city streets; of the Roman and mediaeval city long since buried beneath the metropolis of the Industrial Revolution; of haunted houses and stately homes; of an untold curse; of a unique tribute from a wife to her husband; of the warehouses that became luxurious hotels and upmarket restaurants; of a working mill that has survived and of a green village built on the site of some of the Industrial Revolution's most sordid sufferings; of a hidden church; and a Czech religious retreat; of how Marks & Spencer began; of music halls and Saturday nights in the early millscapes. Some parts of hidden Manchester can be found with careful searching; other parts were lost long ago to the ravages of time or encroaching urbanisation.

Glynis Cooper
June 2004

The Lonely Cottages

TWO ISOLATED cottages standing beside a moorland road, a lonely straight moorland road leading away towards Oldham, the 'old hamlet' in the hills. Ancoats – *ana cots* – the lonely cottages. These small outlying cottages stood at the edge of the estate of an old manor house, a black and white timbered building known as Ancoats Hall. The surrounding woodlands were full of roe deer and wild boar. In summer fields of corn waved and rippled their yellow ears, nodding to each other in the sunshine, while the hedgerows were thick with wild raspberries, and later, after the harvest in September, with blackberries.

It was, someone once wrote, 'an old golden land' where life was dependent upon the agricultural cycle, as it had always been; and where custom and tradition, folklore and legend, festivals and fairs, reflected this ancient way of life.

Within a decade, however, during the 1790s, this centuries-old way of life was brought to a sudden and brutal end, extinguished in a moment of time by the advent of a phenomenon the world had not seen before: the Industrial Revolution.

Ancoats is bounded by Oldham Street, Great Ancoats Street, the Ashton Canal and Pollard Street. There were several important early mills. Murray Mill, built in 1798, was a steam-driven mill and one of the first mills to be built in Ancoats. At first, like their neighbours, McConnell and Kennedy, Adam and George Murray were spinning machine makers, before deciding to use their machines themselves for spinning. As the cotton industry grew the Murray brothers extended their first mill (the Old Mill), adding Decker Mill in 1801, followed by New Mill on Jersey Street in 1804. The three mills were then joined by a series of smaller buildings to form a courtyard which was entered by a 'Great Gate'. Within the courtyard a canal basin was built and linked by a tunnel to the Rochdale Canal. Other early Ancoats mills included

Plush new apartments and offices in old mills and warehouses by the canal side at Piccadilly Basin.

Jersey Mill and the Beehive Mill, both on Jersey Street, and Pin Mill on Pin Mill Brow.

The intensive use of Ancoats and its neighbours by the cotton mills took its toll:

> *A thick black smoke covers the city. The sun appears like a disc without any rays. In this semi-daylight 300,000 people work ceaselessly. A thousand noises rise amidst this unending damp and dark labyrinth... the footsteps of a busy crowd, the crunching wheels of machines, the shriek of steam from the boilers, the regular beat of looms, the heavy rumble of carts, these are the only noises from which you can never escape in these dark half-lit streets...*
> (Alexis de Toqueville, *Oeuvres Complêtes*, 1835)

Ten years later Friedrich Engels was visibly shocked by what Ancoats had become:

...included under the name Ancoats, stand the largest mills of Manchester lining the canals, colossal six and seven-storied buildings towering with their slender chimneys far above the low cottages of the workers. The population of the district, consists, therefore, chiefly of mill-hands, and in the worst streets, of hand-weavers. The streets nearest the heart of the town are the oldest, and consequently, the worst...

> (F. Engels, *The Condition of the Working Class in England*, 1845)

Engels was not the only writer to describe life in the area at that time:

...operative Manchester is up and stirring before six... the streets in the neighbourhood of the mills are thronged with men, women and children flocking to their labour... The factory bell rings from five minutes before six until the hour strikes. Then... the engine starts and the day's work begins. Those who are behind six... are fined two pence; and... after... a very short time of grace, the doors are locked... I cannot say much for the cleanliness of the workpeople. They have an essentially greasy look... men and women appeared to be more or less in a negative sanitary condition.

> (*Manchester and the Textile Districts in 1849*, Angus Bethune Reach. Aspin, *c.*1972. Helmshore Local History Society)

Ancoats has been immortalised by Howard Spring in his novels *Fame is the Spur* and *My Son, My Son*, and in *The Manchester Man* by Mrs Linnaeus Banks. Walk up Ducie Street and back along Piccadilly and into the Piccadilly Basin, which is a kind of gateway to Ancoats. The horizon is a millscape of old mills and disused warehouses. From the car park it is possible to see the partly culverted Rochdale Canal by the old Dale Street warehouse. Here still is the essence of 'Cottonopolis' in the world's first industrial suburb, which is now poised to become the world's first urban village.

The East Manchester urban regeneration scheme has planned to revitalise Ancoats and the neighbouring millscape suburbs of Ardwick, Beswick, Bradford, Miles Platting and Openshaw. There are already streets of cleaned and refurbished mill-workers cottages in Ancoats where communities are being re-established. Canals and towpaths are being landscaped. Old mill buildings are being re-utilised as music studios, clubs, and apartments and there is a school of music in one former Ancoats mill. The windows of Murray's Mills now have gaily painted shutters, colour-coded floor by floor.

Dales Warehouse, built 1806, at Piccadilly Basin, Ancoats. The internal docks and external goods doors are still clearly visible.

Contrast this with a description of Ancoats during the 1840s:

...a wide-lying labyrinth of small dingy streets, narrow unsunned courts terminating in gloomy culs de sac, and adorned with a central sloppy gutter. Every score of yards or so you catch sight of one of the second and third class mills, with its cinder paved courtyard and its steaming engine house. Shabby looking chapels, here and there, rise with infinitesimal Gothic arches and ornaments, amid the grimy nakedness of the factories. Now a rail-road, upon its understructure of arches, passes over the roofs; anon, you cross a canal, with wharfs and coal-yards and clusters of unmoving barges...

(Manchester and the Textile Districts in 1849, Angus Bethune Reach. Aspin, *c.*1972, Helmshore Local History Society)

One of the 'shabby' churches is also included in the regeneration scheme. St Peter's Church was built on Jersey Street in 1859 but fell into disuse after a century of worship and is now being restored. Not so fortunate was St Andrew's Church, built in 1829 on Travis Street, though it survived until 1961. During demolition workmen were badly spooked when four coffins were found sealed in a secret tomb beneath the altar. The identity of the occupants and why they were placed in their secret tomb remains unknown. The placing of the tomb beneath the altar greatly reduced the risk of it ever being discovered; at least to the 19th-century clerical mind which could not have dreamed of the destruction of the 20th century or the rapidly declining interest in church attendance.

Archimedes at UMIST

UNDER ONE of the railway arches just a few yards away from the Vimto monument in Granby Row is a larger-than-life model of Archimedes sitting in his bathtub. Archimedes' expression suggests he is equally startled at being discovered thus and his bathtub seems just a trifle modern for an Ancient Greek but it is a striking sculpture placed there by UMIST. As Archimedes was a major scientific scholar and perhaps one of the first 'true' mechanics, it is entirely appropriate that he should grace an innovative Institute of Science and Technology.

UMIST was founded at the Bridgewater Arms in 1824 by Manchester's business community. It was initially a Mechanics Institute. The first UMIST buildings on Sackville Street stood close to the manufacturing unit where Vimto was created and to the railway arches under which Archimedes sits, forever about to get out of his bath, his eyes transfixed by something on the far horizon.

In 1919 UMIST graduate Sir Arthur Brown became the first man to fly the Atlantic; and in 1951 Sir John Cockcroft, another UMIST graduate, was awarded the Nobel Prize for Physics for 'transmuting the atom'. UMIST was also '...the first UK university to offer chemical engineering undergraduate degree programmes; the first to offer courses in management and marketing; and the first to establish an industrial liaison unit...'

Archimedes (287-212 BC) was born in Syracuse and died there when the Romans captured the city. He was a renowned Greek scientist and mathematician whose specialisms were mechanics and hydrostatics. He proved that '...a body plunged into a fluid loses as much of its weight as is equal to the weight of an equal volume of the fluid...' (*Chambers Biographical Dictionary*, 1984). This probably explains why swimmers feel that their bodies are lighter when they are in the water; and why the sculpture under the arches portrays Archimedes emerging from his bath tub.

Archimedes rising from his bath tub beneath a railway arch facing UMIST (off Granby Row).

Archimedes also invented the 'endless screw' and the 'Archimedes screw', which was a spiral pump for drawing up water; as well as siege-breaking war engines, which acted like great catapults, and a 'compound pulley system' for moving heavy weights. Geometry was his real passion, however, and legend says that he was killed by a Roman soldier because he refused to obey an order to report to the Roman commander, Marcellus, until he had completed working out some geometrical problem. On his tomb there was '...a cylinder circumscribing a sphere and his result of the ratio of the two...'; a fitting epitaph for a truly great mathematician.

Castlefield

BEFORE THE Romans arrived in the north-west the Manchester area was controlled by the Brigantes, a Celtic tribe renowned for their skills in guerrilla warfare. The countryside was quite heavily wooded at that period and full of wild boar, deer and wolves. In keeping with Celtic tradition the Brigantes chose the red sandstone outcrop, where the River Irk and the River Irwell merged, as their main settlement. The elevated nature of the site gave them a good defensive position and water supplies were easily accessible. The woods offered fertile hunting grounds and the local soil was reasonably productive for growing crops. There was a good proportion of oak trees among the woodlands, which suited the Brigantes because oak trees and water were prerequisites for the Druids, the Celtic priests, to perform their ancient rites and rituals.

Café society along the Rochdale Canal underneath the railway arches near Deansgate Station and Gaythorn close to Castlefield.

Jackson's Wharf, a former canal warehouse, now a fish restaurant at Castlefield.

Barça, a celebrity bar beneath the railway arches at Castlefield.

When the Romans arrived around AD 70 they chose a lower spur of land just across 'town' at the confluence of the River Irwell and the River Medlock, to build their fort. This was in accordance with contemporary Roman military thinking and echoed the arrangements at Glossop in Derbyshire some 12 to 15 miles to the east. Here the Brigantes had firm control of what is today known as Mouselow (Mous Hlaw), a rocky outcrop close to water which offered an excellent defensive position. The Romans had settled on a lower spur of sandstone across the valley close to the River Etherow and established a fort called Edrotalia; known as Melandra in more recent times.

Merchants Warehouse at Castlefield showing 'twin shipping holes' to internal docks. The building now houses apartments and offices.

Agricola, who was responsible for building Edrotalia, built a much larger fort, about five acres in size, at Castlefield in AD 79. It was called Mamuciam. *Mam* is the Celtic name for 'hill', especially a rounded hill whose general shape is similar to that of a human female breast. The town later became known as Mamceastre, *ceaster* derived from the Latin word for a walled town which had originally been a Roman settlement or station. The name of Castlefield comes from mediaeval times when the derelict and overgrown fort was known simply as the Castle-in-the-Field, which was later shortened to Castlefield.

There were three main phases of fort building at Castlefield. The first fort (AD 79–*c*.AD 110–125) was built of timber and turf. There were two defensive ditches on three sides; the river to the south providing the remaining defensive measure. Opposite the river the north gate was guarded by a couple of wooden towers. A larger fort was built around AD 160 and the north gate blocked by a ditch. The final phase saw a stone fort of similar plan replace the timber and turf structure in about AD 200, which remained in use until the Romans abandoned Britain in AD 410. Seventeen changes were made to the defensive ditches of this last fort, suggesting turbulent times during the last 200 years of the Roman occupation.

Evidence of metalworking and pottery making has been found in the *vicus* or civilian settlement adjacent to the fort. The Brigantes, while hating the Romans, were not averse to trading with them and the *vicus* developed into a trading centre of some importance during the Roman occupation. The Brigantian queen, Cartimandua, was also known to have co-operated with the Romans, but this may have been born out of a desire to rid herself of a husband she hated rather than for motives of trade or appeasement. The Romans obliged by keeping her husband, Caractacus, in chains and under house arrest in Rome until his death. Cartimandua then married Venutius, the Roman 'overlord' of York; but he later betrayed her in turn by switching sides to support the Brigantes.

The legend of Queen Cartimandua has survived for nearly 2,000 years. In the 19th or early 20th century a stone head in a supposed likeness of Cartimandua was found near Manchester. There is still a Celtic stone head tradition in North Derbyshire, West Yorkshire and parts of the Manchester area. The Celts believed that if a likeness of a person was carved in stone then that person could continue to communicate with the living after death. Some of the stone heads carved in the Celtic tradition are held by Manchester Museum on Oxford Road; but Cartimandua, sold to a Derbyshire dealer some years ago, is not among them.

Although the site was robbed for building stone, it was, in the end, neither

Mural of Roman cavalry and infantry under a railway bridge at Castlefield.

time nor the Romans which destroyed the fort at Castlefield – it was the
Industrial Revolution. Roads, railways and canals destroyed most of the
surface remains of the fort and also covered the area of the *vicus*. All that
remains are a few hummocks and a section of wall beneath one of the railway
arches. Along the wall, stretching into the depths of the arches, someone has
painted a mural of foot soldiers of the Roman Legions marching towards the
area of the fort led by the Roman cavalry. The mural has been skilfully
executed so that the column of foot soldiers stretches away from the viewer
and back into time until they can no longer be seen.

A small area of the former fort, with part of a curtain wall and a modern
interpretation of a Roman watch tower, together with the North Gate, has
been reconstructed. The North Gate looks out across a dismal park instead
of the woodlands and countryside of Roman times; the wild boar and the
wolves are long gone. An inscription has been added to the gate commemorating troops from Spain, Austria and Romania who served at Mamucium in
around AD 200, together with their Centurion, Lucius Senecianus Martius.
From the Guardroom above the gateway there is a wonderful distance view
towards the tower blocks of south Manchester. In Roman times there would
have been all round distance views (now blocked by modern buildings) and
it is easy to appreciate why the Romans would have chosen this spot.

Today much of Castlefield is commemorated as an Urban Heritage Park,
the first in Britain. There is a canal basin criss-crossed by railway lines and

*Reconstruction of part of
the former Roman fort at
Castlefield. The watch
tower looks down on
white canopies, part of
modern café society at
Castlefield.*

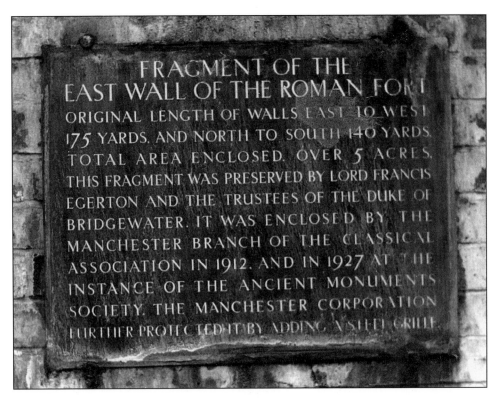

FRAGMENT OF THE
EAST WALL OF THE ROMAN FORT
ORIGINAL LENGTH OF WALLS EAST TO WEST
175 YARDS. AND NORTH TO SOUTH 140 YARDS.
TOTAL AREA ENCLOSED. OVER 5 ACRES.
THIS FRAGMENT WAS PRESERVED BY LORD FRANCIS
EGERTON AND THE TRUSTEES OF THE DUKE OF
BRIDGEWATER. IT WAS ENCLOSED BY THE
MANCHESTER BRANCH OF THE CLASSICAL
ASSOCIATION IN 1912. AND IN 1927 AT THE
INSTANCE OF THE ANCIENT MONUMENTS
SOCIETY. THE MANCHESTER CORPORATION
FURTHER PROTECTED IT BY ADDING A STEEL GRILLE

surrounded by former warehouses. During the 1760s the Duke of Bridge-water built a canal from his Worsley coal mines to Castlefield. As canal transportation grew the Ashton and Rochdale canals were built and joined the Duke of Bridgewater's canal at Castlefield. By the mid 19th-century warehouses and mills had been built along the canals and a network of railway lines created the Spaghetti Junction of their day.

The Castlefield Basin now stages a variety of outdoor events including entertainments, craft festivals, an annual carnival and an annual narrowboat rally, when lovingly restored and gaily painted barges of all shapes and sizes travel to Castlefield for a late summer weekend of fun and nostalgia. The wharves and quays have been cleaned, restored and landscaped. Warehouses have been converted into apartments, hotels, restaurants, pubs and clubs. One of the best known is Dukes 92, named after the Duke of Bridgewater whose industrial efforts did so much to destroy the old Castlefield. Its clean, pleasant white interior design belies its grimy industrial heritage. Even the cobbled street outside is clean. Barça is the celebrity pub. Jackson's Wharf has kept more to the tradition of the area and retains its own name. Seafood dishes are a speciality here as one might expect of a former 'waterfront' building.

The Middle Warehouse was built 1828–31 at the head of the Middle Basin. Like the Merchants Warehouse it had twin 'shipping holes' to internal docks and external goods doors with hoists. Today there is a wooden bridge across the canal basin to allow easy pedestrian access to both sides of the building. Most of the Middle Warehouse has been transformed into luxury waterside apartments, but one of the most surprising conversions is that of the ground floor of the warehouse into an upmarket restaurant named Choice. Here there is parquet flooring; thick carpets; elegant glass and silverware on the tables and a grand piano in the bar. Dishes like smoked trout with piccalilli and quails eggs; halloumi and asparagus on chickpea couscous; hot duck salad; or guinea fowl and game chips; are unusual, tasty and imaginative, but about as different as you could get from the simple fare of the former occupants who considered bread and cheese, bacon and cabbage, potatoes, and an occasional hot pot as their staple and adequate diet.

Nearby, the former early Grocers Warehouse is commemorated by a semi-circle of giant rusting cog wheel. It bears a circular plaque with the following inscription:

Grocers Warehouse

Built on the site where coal was first brought to Manchester by canal for the 1st Duke of Bridgewater. The warehouse marks the location where coal was transferred to street level using water wheel driven machinery designed and built by James Brindley. The delivery of cheap coal marked the beginning of the Industrial Revolution and helped to establish Manchester as a principal manufacturing centre.

As a result of increasing trade and success of the scheme a warehouse for the storage of provisions was constructed on the site of the coal wharf. The original building was demolished in 1960 and the partial reconstruction which incorporated a water wheel driven hoist was completed in 1967.

Duke's 92 at Castlefield – restaurant and pub in a former warehouse named after the Duke of Bridgewater.

GROCERS
WAREHOUSE

Site of former Grocers Warehouse at Castlefield.

In the early 1770s the Grocers Warehouse was built beside the coal wharf. Five storeys high, the warehouse had five window bays facing the canal and a single entrance two storeys high. Boats entered the building here for unloading at the internal dock where there was a water-powered hoist. In 1793 the warehouse was extended and doubled in length. The original warehouse was demolished in 1960.

The Merchants Warehouse was built off Catalan Square in 1825. The red-brick building stands alongside the canal rather than in the basin itself. The warehouse had 'paired shipping holes' leading to internal docks although there were also goods doors and external hoists. Despite being damaged by fire in 1971 the building survived and was converted into luxury offices and apartments five years later. Weeping willow trees have now been planted close to the Merchants Warehouse.

Chetham's Library

JUST TO the north of the Cathedral lie the Cathedral Gardens, once formally laid out gardens, now a large pleasant square of green with fountains at the heart of the former mediaeval city of Manchester where people can stroll, talk, relax or sun themselves. The Triangle lies to the east; Victoria Street (leading to Victoria Station) to the west. On the north-east side is the ultra-modern glass Urbis, a museum devoted to the history of urban life on a global scale and a monument to 21st-century ideas of architecture and heritage. Facing Urbis across the Gardens on the north-west side is the late mediaeval complex of Chetham's, a monument in its own way to the architecture of its own time, the antithesis of Urbis in time, space and concept.

Shortly after the Norman Conquest of 1066 Manchester became a barony and a 'baronial hall' or manor house was built on the site where Chetham's now stands. In 1421, Thomas de la Warre, the Lord of Manchester, obtained the status of Collegiate Church for the old 10th-century parish church of St Mary's. He rebuilt the manor house on the lines of a small college, which would house a warden, eight Fellows, four clerks and six lay choristers. These buildings, despite a chequered history, survive today.

The College was closed down in 1547 after the Dissolution of the Monasteries; re-founded during the reign of the Catholic Queen Mary Tudor (1553–8); closed down again when she died, and eventually re-established as Christ's College in 1578 under Queen Elizabeth I. In 1595 the Queen appointed Dr John Dee as warden of the College.

John Dee was an intelligent man who was Cambridge educated and, after gaining his degree, he met the famous map-maker Gerald Mercator when he travelled with other scholars to Holland. Dee became a renowned mathematician, astronomer, astrologer and an alchemist who dabbled in crystal gazing

*Chetham's mediaeval
gatehouse, photographed
in 1955.* (Manchester
Archives & Local Studies,
Central Library)

and necromancy. He spent much of his life searching for the Philosopher's Stone and he claimed to have found the elixir of life at Glastonbury Abbey.

He made friends with the Byron family, who owned a 12th-century moated manor house at Clayton, about half an hour's ride from the College, and he dined with them on a regular basis. As the firelight flickered on the wooden panels of the walls and the family, with their guests, tucked into roast meats and boiled fish, game pies and salads and sweetmeats, washed down with plenty of good wine and ale, it is tempting to wonder if Dr Dee ever talked about any of his theories and researches into alchemy. Alchemy was a mediaeval forerunner of chemistry but in Elizabethan times it was often regarded as witchcraft.

John Dee seemed rather an unlikely choice for the post of warden, but he had made enemies through his work in alchemy and the Queen had deemed it politically expedient for him to leave London for a while. Dr Dee held the post of warden at Christ's (the former Collegiate) College in Manchester for eight years before returning to London in 1604.

During the English Civil War (1640–9) the buildings were used as a prison and an arsenal, becoming semi-derelict afterwards; but around 1651

negotiations were begun for purchase of the buildings by Humphrey Chetham.

Humphrey Chetham was born at Crumpsall Hall in 1580 and received an education at Manchester Grammar School. He was a wealthy merchant and became High Sheriff of Lancashire in 1635. It was Chetham's ambition to do something which would be of benefit to scholars but which would also help poorer children to gain an education. He died in 1653 while negotiations for the purchase of the former College were still continuing, but he left strict and concise instructions in his will. Most of his fortune was '...to be used to endow a hospital for the maintenance and education of forty poor boys...' and he also left £1,000 to '...adapt and equip part of the library for the use of scholars...' plus a further sum of £200 for chained libraries in five local churches.

The former College dormitories, ranged along two long wings, the Priests Wing and the Mary Chapel Wing, were adapted for housing the book collections. The collections are catalogued chronologically and the books are kept in dark polished wooden presses (bookcases), most of which have open lattice-work doors. Chetham had insisted that the library books should be chained, but this practice was discontinued in the 1740s and what must be some of the earliest known security gates were installed.

The Reading Room is in what would probably have been the manorial master bedroom; a comfortable room of roughly square proportions with a vaulted black and white timbered ceiling and wooden panelling on the walls. There are windows looking out across the former site of the apple orchard (between the northern border of the Cathedral's consecrated ground and the

southern boundary of Chetham's courtyard there was a street known as the Apple Market) and down Hunts Bank towards the Irk (before it was culverted) which supplied fish for the College until the waters were poisoned by the industrial pollution of 'Cottonopolis'.

Above the fireplace hangs a portrait of Humphrey Chetham and above that is a large heraldic work featuring the Chetham arms, flanked by books and

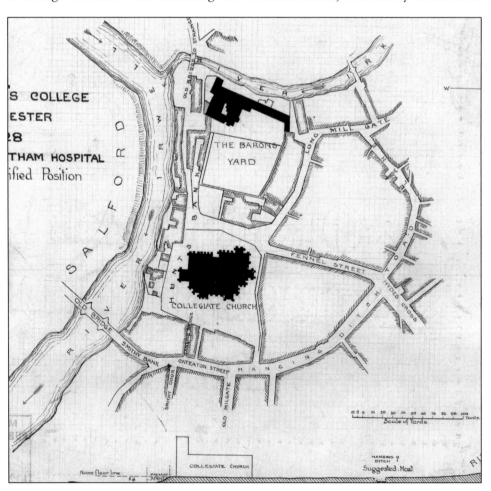

The former Cathedral Gardens showing the ultra-modern Urbis museum of urban history and the Printworks complex.

'torches of learning', and two beautifully fashioned raised carvings of 'a cock and a pelican feeding her young'. The Gorton chained library is held in a locked wooden bookcase in one corner of the room. It is a small collection of theological works, each individually chained to its bookshelf. The chain links are long and narrow but effective. In the middle of the room is a large oval wooden table around which are ranked 14 chairs. This is where library users read and research books, documents and manuscripts; and it was here, in this quiet warm oasis from another age, that Karl Marx and Friedrich Engels sat and worked together on their *Communist Manifesto,* which would completely revolutionise 20th-century world politics.

Chetham's Library has been buying books, manuscripts and archives since 1655. Early specialist subjects included theology, law, history, medicine and science. Among the local collections are archives of the infamous massacre at Peterloo in 1819 and that of Belle Vue Zoo and Gardens (1836–1970). Apart from lions, tea-dances and botanical wonders, one of Belle Vue's more unusual attractions was a visit by Buffalo Bill Cody and his Indian Chiefs in the late 1890s. Individual items of interest held by the Library include a first edition of Sir Isaac Newton's book on the natural philosophy and principles of mathematics (1687); Ben Jonson's copy of *Plato* (1578); and the original manuscript of *The Manchester Man* by Mrs George Linnaeus Banks (1889), which features the Peterloo Massacre.

On the ground floor of Chetham's is the Baronial Hall where Thomas de la Warre and subsequently the members of the College would have dined. In late mediaeval and Tudor times the main meal was taken in the middle of the day. It could consist of several courses and last up to two hours. The Hall has stone walls and a flagged floor and retains its three-part oak screen at the rear, which helped to keep out draughts. Originally the hearth was in the centre of the hall and smoke was drawn up through a simple opening in the roof. The present inglenook-style fireplace is of later date and the 'oriel bay' behind it is 19th century, while the ceiling is now enclosed and vaulted with black and white timbers. Today weekly lunchtime concerts are held in the hall which are attended by members of the public and students from the adjoining Chetham's School of Music.

The library is still open on weekdays for public use. Over the centuries thousands of scholars, researchers and readers have passed through the portals of the dark polished wooden rooms. Guided public tours of the mediaeval College buildings, which also include the Association Room (the former kitchen), the Audit Room and the cloisters, are available and enquiries should be made at the Gatehouse. The cloisters, unusually, are two-storey, and it is here in these stone corridors, with their sloping timbered roofs, which have remained virtually unchanged for almost 600 years, that the echoes of history are strongest. It is almost impossible not to hear the muted tones of past scholars and readers, not to feel the brush of soft material as someone walks past, or not to catch a glimpse of a dark figure hurrying round a corner. Here is the essence of hidden Manchester.

China Town

THE FAMILY home of Beatrix Potter's grandfather, Edmund Potter, stood in Faulkner Street, close to Piccadilly, the heart of the city, and close to Charlotte Street where he established his first merchant's warehouse. It was to Faulkner Street that he brought his new bride, Jessie Crompton, a Lancaster beauty, while he set up their first home together in Greenheys, near Manchester University. Faulkner Street was an integral part of the business community whose warehouses dominated the centre of Manchester throughout the 19th century. Edmund Potter died in 1883 but were he able to return today he would probably be both amazed and excited by the changes which have taken place in Faulkner Street.

Faulkner Street is no longer the heart of an English business community but of a Chinese business community. The street is dominated by a beautiful red and gold Chinese arch, decorated with dragons and phoenixes which are symbols of luck and prosperity. The arch was erected in 1987 and is said to be '...the first true Imperial Chinese arch erected in Europe...' At the same time a Chinese pagoda was built in the street and a Chinese garden was planted. A life-size mural of a Chinese junk on the high seas was painted on

The Chinese arch, 1987. (Manchester Archives & Local Studies, Central Library)

The Chinese pagoda in Faulkner Street, photographed in 1987. (Manchester Archives & Local Studies, Central Library)

a brick wall. It was a celebration of Chinese culture and the making of a Chinese village or town where Chinese people from all over the north-west could congregate; a little piece of China in England.

Increasingly, Chinese emigrants have been coming to England for about 60 years; mostly from Hong Kong or Kowloon, as a result of unfavourable economic changes in their homeland. An industrious and hard-working people, they set up their own businesses. Initially Chinese laundries were popular, laundry being an occupation carried out mainly by Chinese hands on the ships which sailed into Liverpool and London in the 19th century; but with the growth of domestic washing machines in the 1960s the Chinese diversified into restaurants to cater for a fast-growing British demand for Chinese food. There are a number of excellent Chinese restaurants and takeaways in Manchester and its surrounding towns; many of which '...do their own thing...'

At Buffet City in a basement off Oxford Road there is the most amazing Chinese buffet served daily, offering a large range of freshly cooked savoury and sweet Chinese dishes kept hot by extremely efficient heating trolleys. Customers pay £5 each and eat their fill. Another Chinese restaurant on Portland Street, close to Faulkner Street, offers Chinese banquets for those with more leisure and more money. There is no menu. The waiter or waitress will ask what food preferences customers have (types of meat, vegetables etc) and the banquet will be tailored to individual requirements. Banquet is an

Wall mural of a Chinese junk in Manchester's China Town, 1988. (Manchester Archives & Local Studies, Central Library)

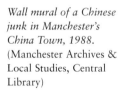

*Chinese arch,
surrounded by former
Victorian warehouses, in
Faulkner Street, the hub
of China Town.*

understatement. There are no different courses in the Western sense. As fast as one dish is finished, more replace it until even the most dedicated eater pleads 'no more!'

As the Chinese population has grown so has the need for Chinese financial and legal services, Chinese medicine shops and health centres, and these are centred around what has come to be known as China Town. Chinese practices such as acupuncture and the ancient art of Feng Shui are becoming increasing popular with Westerners. Edmund Potter's house no longer survives – it has been replaced with a modern office block – but he was a forward-looking and innovative manufacturer and businessman and he would have understood and appreciated progress.

There is also a new Chinese Arts and Cultural Centre, although this is hidden away on Thomas Street in the 'Northern Quarter' of the city centre. It includes a Chinese gallery, a Chinese library and a Chinese tea room, as well as a gift shop where Chinese books, music and paintings are for sale. Central Library on St Peter's Square has recognised the importance of the Chinese community by setting up a Chinese Library with Chinese staff on the second floor. The Chinese New Year is also celebrated annually in Manchester with thousands of Chinese and non-Chinese people taking part. There are street parties and performers and processions led by the largest dancing dragon in Europe.

Chorlton Ees

THE OLD name for Chorlton-cum-Hardy is Ceorlatun-cum-Ard-Eea; a long name but a simple meaning: the settlement of ceorls (Saxon freemen) by trees near the water. The River Mersey (Maeres-Eea, meaning boundary water) runs along the edge of Chorlton parish and the original settlement was probably either on or close to the water meadows.

The sprawling fingers of the millscapes never managed to reach as far as Chorlton-cum-Hardy so the area was able to retain some of its quaint old worldness until well into the 20th century. It was a farming community where crop cycles and breeding livestock and old country traditions fashioned the way of life for centuries. Some of the countryside has been preserved and a Water Park has been established under the Red Rose Forest scheme.

The Water Park itself occupies land once owned by Barlow Hall Farm in an area known locally as Chorlton Ees. The River Mersey runs through fields and small copses and there is a large lake which was made when gravel was excavated for the M63 motorway in the 1970s. The woodlands, water meadows and surrounding grasslands have provided an ideal and much-needed habitat for a variety of wildlife, flora and fauna; while the lake is stocked with pike, carp, tench, roach, perch and bream.

From May–September the Water Park offers canoeing, sailing and windsurfing for people of all levels of ability. There are also raft races and regattas although these are usually for charity. A number of outdoor activities are available including cycling, horse riding, orienteering, fishing, or just strolling along the network of country paths listening to the birdsong.

Chorlton Ees has been termed 'urban countryside' – modern jargon for a rural retreat within the city. Basically the Saxons knew how to pick a pretty spot for their settlements and this has been appreciated by successive generations. Listening to birdsong and watching butterflies stretching their delicate wings in warm afternoon sunshine, while children practice jumping their ponies in the quiet fields close to the river, is a centuries-old pastime and it is hard to believe that the bustling heart of the industrial metropolis, which has become the second city of England, lies just down the road.

Clayton Hall

CLAYTON HALL, a moated manor house, was built in the 12th century on land owned by the Byron or Buron family. The hall was rebuilt during the Tudor period. A bell which hangs 'in the wooded turret at the south end of the Hall' was rumoured to have been 'taken from the old parish Church of Manchester during its rebuilding in the 15th century'. Dr John Dee, the Tudor mathematician, alchemist, and astrologer to Queen Elizabeth I, was a friend of the Byron family and dined with them regularly during his wardenship of the Collegiate Church (1595–1603).

Humphrey Chetham, born in 1580, would have been a teenager when Dr Dee arrived in Manchester to take up the wardenship. Chetham was no stranger to Clayton Hall. He loved the house and he was a frequent visitor. It is quite likely that he met Dr Dee there and he would have been fascinated by tales of the older man's scientific and spiritual searchings.

The Byron family (ancestors of the renowned poet, Lord Byron) remained at the hall until they sold it to Humphrey Chetham, possibly its most famous resident, in 1620. Chetham lived there until his death in 1653. In his will he left money for the foundation of Chetham's Library in Manchester, which was the first free public library in Britain, and for chained libraries to be established in five local churches. He also left money to found a Bluecoat School which was named Chetham's Hospital, now known as Chetham's School of Music.

A tragic legend dating from the time of the Crusades is attached to the family. Sir Hugo de Buron set out on the Third Crusade leaving his beautiful young wife at the hall. Time passed and Sir Hugo did not return. Finally his wife was told that he had been killed in battle. She was devastated and within a few months she had died of a broken heart. Her funeral procession was met by a knight on his way home from the Crusades who turned out to be Sir Hugo himself. Grief-stricken, he renounced his knighthood, surrendered his weapons and gave up fighting. He made a full confession and then became a monk, taking his vows in the remote isolation of Kersal Cell on Kersal Moor.

Clayton Hall survives and is the only example of a moated manor house in

Black and white timbered
Clayton Hall, 1900.
(Manchester Archives &
Local Studies, Central
Library)

Manchester. The upper part of the house retains its black and white Tudor timbers, but the lower part is brick faced. Today it is a private house, surrounded by a modern housing estate built in the former grounds. The view of the hall from Ashton Old Road is almost totally blocked by St Cross Church and the aspects are thus much diminished. Sir Hugo would be shocked if he were to return to his family home today.

The hall had a ghost of course, but an unexpected one. It might be thought that the spectre who haunted the old Tudor building would be that of either the lovelorn Sir Hugo or his wife; or perhaps even Humphrey Chetham, returned to stroll in the grounds of his beloved house. It was none of these but a rather more mundane if mischievous boggart. The boggart was finally laid by a local vicar who then declared 'whilst ivy and holly are green, Clayton Hall boggart shall no more be seen.'

Didsbury Haunts

T HE 'GATES TO HELL' seemed an odd choice of name for the wrought-
iron gates topped by a rather fine eagle which stood at the entrance to the
nice old-fashioned garden. The road outside at one time took its name from
these gates as well. However, the word 'Hell' did not relate to the gates, but
rather to what they guarded.

Didsbury lies in the southern suburbs of the city and is reached by the
No.42 bus route from Piccadilly Gardens. St James's Church in Didsbury
stands near the River Mersey on the site of a wooden chapel which was 'of
antiquity beyond memory' in 1235. In 1620 the Chapel was rebuilt and a
tower was added so that it became like the church with which Didsbury
residents are familiar today. St James's was extended and rebuilt in 1842; and
further restored in 1855.

A parsonage for St James's was built next to the Old Cock Inn on Spring
Hill Lane (now Stenner Lane). There used to be a cock pit in the yard of the
inn; hence the name; and cock fights took place there regularly. In 1745,
according to legend, the troops of Bonnie Prince Charlie were an enthusiastic

The Old Parsonage, home of Fletcher Moss (now a museum), Didsbury, 1890. (Manchester Archives & Local Studies, Central Library)

The Roman well at the Old Parsonage, 1900. (Manchester Archives & Local Studies, Central Library)

audience at the cock fights and spent well. However, if all the legends of Bonnie Prince Charlie and his men in Manchester were true they would have been having such a social whirl that they would never have found time to march for Derby on their way to London.

By the time the parsonage was built the cock fights had mainly ceased but life was far from peaceful for those who lived in the house. They were woken during the night by bells ringing, noises, thumps and bangs which seemed to come from within the house. Servants refused to sleep there overnight. Some claimed that they had seen transparent wraiths floating through the trees of the graveyard and the parsonage garden; perhaps the ghosts of long dead victims of the Black Death, which had visited Didsbury in 1352. Things became so bad that 'clergymen of all denominations were hired to lay the spirits'. Nothing worked. In 1850 the parsonage was finally abandoned and became known as the Old Parsonage.

The house lay empty for some time until 1865 when it was bought by local writer and historian, Fletcher Moss. He was sceptical of the claims and described the Parsonage 'as having no cellars, no ventilation or lift shafts where howling winds could be mistaken for ghosts'. However, his terrier dog, Gomer, had other ideas. He frequently growled at 'something standing in the doorway of the house', his bristly hair and tail standing on end, and Fletcher Moss finally decided that 'Gomer's sixth sense had probably detected a "pre-historic spirit" for which the house had become notorious.'

He doesn't say who or what the 'pre-historic spirit' was, but it would have been something which had been there long before the house was built. It may have been an ancient elemental spirit often found close to woods and water,

From left to right: Didsbury Hotel; St James's Church; Gates of Hell; Ye Old Cock Inn, 1900. (Manchester Archives & Local Studies, Central Library)

or a legacy from Celtic times. In prehistoric times (i.e. before the Romans) Didsbury was a heavily wooded fertile area through which the River Mersey flowed, and it would have been settled by the Celtic peoples who arrived in Britain in around 500 BC. The Celts worshipped trees, water, the earth, all things natural. Their priests, the Druids, invoked powerful passions and powerful spirits.

A Roman well head stands in the gardens of the Old Parsonage and it has been suggested that there may have been a Roman settlement in Didsbury since the discovery of a Roman coin from the reign of Antoninus Pius near Millgate Lane. If the Romans were in the area there would almost certainly have been a Celtic trading post in the vicinity, if not a sizeable farming community.

Fletcher Moss was a prolific writer on Didsbury and its legends. Although a century or more old his books make fascinating reading, although he never managed to solve the mystery of the Parsonage. People in the village were terrified of the house, but despite mysterious happenings, Fletcher Moss lived there for over 40 years. In 1902 he bought the wrought-iron gates and the eagle from the Spread Eagle in Manchester and erected them at the entrance to his garden. They became known locally as 'the gates to Hell' because of the Parsonage's reputation.

The Old Parsonage wasn't the only haunted house in Didsbury that Fletcher Moss discovered. Researching a book on Manchester folklore he discovered a story about a house known only as the Swivel House. However, he was refused permission to publish the story and since then the house has been renamed several times and rebuilt, so that today no one knows its exact location. Later he did write about it, in chilling detail, but gave no identifying details of the places or people involved.

...each night at about midnight a lady would appear in one of the bedrooms dressed in frills and furbelows, powders and pattens [an old fashioned shoe], and a gown of green brocade rustling like autumn leaves... she lingered by the foot of the bed for a few moments before silently fading into the wall. Legend rumoured that she was the sweetheart of a previous owner who had been a very wealthy man and that she had been walled up alive because she knew too much about how he had come by his wealth. During 19th-century alterations to the house 'a secret chamber' was discovered in the chimney stack containing the decaying remains of an old chair and table, and chicken bones...

After the death of Fletcher Moss the Old Parsonage eventually became the Old Parsonage Museum, specialising in pottery and porcelain displays. It was described as a '...small hidden-away former art gallery which was devoted entirely to depictions of scenes and events local to Manchester...' Unfortunately this gallery is now closed; but the Gardens are still open to the public.

The Fletcher Moss Gardens, as they are known, were given to Manchester Corporation by Fletcher Moss in 1914. The Gardens have '...a small orchid house, many rare tree specimens [including palms, lime and weeping ash which were recorded by Fletcher Moss with dates and measurements] a rose garden and a rich and extensive collection of herbaceous plants...' Climbing plants include honeysuckle, Virginia creeper and passion flower; and there are 'cottage garden flowers' such as marigolds, lilies, borage and rue.

The Old Cock Inn, minus its cockpit, still stands adjacent and is a popular haunt with students during the summer months. The Didsbury Hotel, shown standing opposite the 'gates of Hell' in the early 20th century, remains a hotel, although the cobbled street of 1900 which ran in front of the hotel is now a large grassy area shared by patrons of the hotel bar and the Old Cock Inn.

The local student population is increasing and Didsbury has created a village and café society which is a welcome oasis from the inner-city shopping complexes. There is no heavy industry in Didsbury; it escaped the mills and the worst excesses of the Industrial Revolution. The main village street is spacious and full of pavement cafés which nevertheless have plenty of indoor accommodation in easy chairs or seating at pine scrubbed tables with candles in bottles for when the weather is inclement. There are pubs, clubs, tapas bars, a delightful delicatessen and cheap strawberries can be found even out of season. Apart from more rain and heavier traffic Didsbury has distinct echoes of the Rue Mouffetard on the Left Bank in Paris.

The Textile King

MANCHESTER Town Hall on Albert Square is adorned with statues, standing in niches above head height, of those who helped to shape the history of the town. Hidden away on the north side, which faces Princess Street, one of the statues is that of Edward III. A distant 14th-century king may not be thought to have had very much influence on the history of Manchester at all, but, ultimately, he was the man responsible for Manchester becoming the centre of the world textile industry 500 years after he died.

Edward III, who became king in 1327, was an intelligent man with a good grasp of economics. In the 21st century he would have made an excellent Chancellor of the Exchequer. During mediaeval times England had a thriving woollen industry. The king realised that if woven woollen cloth could be exported, instead of just woollen yarn, wool would be a much more valuable commodity.

Unfortunately the weaving skills of the native English were not good enough to produce woven cloth for export. Edward had been particularly impressed by the skills of the Flemish weavers when he was away fighting on the Continent. Now he was king he officially invited a number of them to settle in England and to teach the English people their weaving skills.

There were two large centres of the woollen industry in Edward's day. One in East Anglia, centred on Norwich; the other in the north-west, centred around Manchester, Preston and Lancaster. Many of the new immigrants remained in East Anglia, but a number made the arduous journey north. One group went to Ordsall at the request of Sir John de Radclyffe of Ordsall Hall who also admired their skills and whom Edward was rewarding for 'services rendered' in the recent wars.

The Flemish weavers were skilled in weaving flax (for linen); fustian (a mixture of cotton and linen); and silk. Two hundred years later their descendants would be joined by Huguenots escaping persecution in France. The Huguenots were skilled weavers as well and their combined efforts put Manchester on the textile map. Dutch and Walloon immigrants of the 1500s were also skilled in making fustian and weaving silk fabric.

Statue of Edward III (who was largely responsible for starting Manchester's textile industry) in a niche on the north side of the Town Hall facing Princess Street.

Towards the end of the Tudor period the city had become well known for its 'Manchester cottons' (a napped woollen weave) and its 'small wares' (ribbons, garters, braids, laces etc.); although it was to be the silk industry which laid the foundations for the incredible phenomena in the 19th century that would become known as 'Cottonopolis'.

Cotton was being manufactured in the Manchester area from about 1680 when the East India Company were busy importing colourful Indian cottons. At this time much of the trading was done by 'chapmen' who stored their wares in the back rooms of convenient inns. As cotton imports and exports increased rapidly, a cotton exchange was established, Manchester being the first town to have such an institution.

Literary inspirations of the millscapes: the Gaskells and the Potters

ELIZABETH GASKELL lost her mother when she was nine and she was then brought up by her aunt in Knutsford, not far from Manchester. Knutsford later became the model for *Cranford* in her popular novel of that name. Elizabeth's uncle, Dr Peter Holland, lived close by. It was his sister, Eliza, who had been her mother. He had a dour countenance but he seems to have been quite a kindly man. The character of Dr Gibson in Elizabeth Gaskell's novel *Wives and Daughters* is based on her uncle.

Dr Holland was the doctor for Quarry Bank Mill at Styal a few miles away. His job was to look after the 100 apprentices that Samuel Greg employed to work at Quarry Bank Mill and he often took the young Elizabeth with him. She saw at first hand the illnesses and injuries suffered by the mill apprentices, some of whom were as young as seven. It was her first introduction to the millscapes which would later feature so prominently in her books.

When she was 22 Elizabeth met and married William Gaskell, who was the Minister for Cross Street Unitarian Chapel. In 1850 they moved to 84 Plymouth Grove, a large Regency family house (now a Grade II listed building) on the edge of Chorlton-on-Medlock. It is not far from Nelson Street, which was the home of the Pankhurst family towards the end of the 19th century. Visitors to her home included Charles Dickens and Charlotte Brontë, whose biography she wrote. A collection of her work is held by Cross

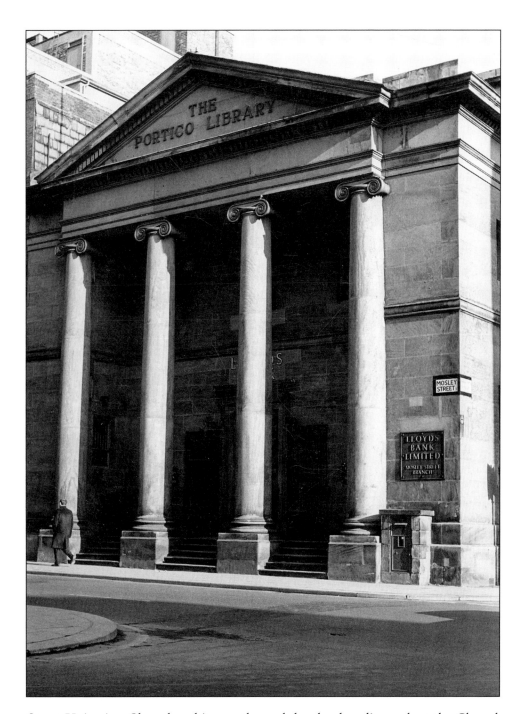

Street Unitarian Chapel and it was through her husband's work at the Chapel that she met the Potter family.

Edmund Potter, like the Gaskells, was a staunch Unitarian. He had been baptised at Cross Street Unitarian Chapel and he worshipped there until he moved to Glossop in Derbyshire to be nearer to his calico printing works. William Gaskell was tutor to Edmund's second son, Rupert, and remained a lifelong friend of both Rupert and Edmund. The Gaskells were frequent visitors at the Potter residence. Rupert Potter became the father of Beatrix Potter, the internationally acclaimed children's writer, and William became like a grandfather to the young Beatrix. Beatrix's grandfather, Edmund, was also a writer, although his work was more serious and concerned with

Elizabeth Gaskell's house, 1959. (Manchester Archives & Local Studies, Central Library)

education, politics and innovative ways of printing calico at his Glossop calico printing works, the largest calico printing works in the world. He was a tall good-looking charismatic man, a self-made mill owner who genuinely believed in the benefits of the millscapes fashioned by the Industrial Revolution. He wrote a pen portrait of a mill town called *Glossop in 1856*:

> *...one general assertion let me make... the workman's, the master's best means for saving must be found in cheap food, cheap cotton or material, and cheap money. The master has, of course, all larger surplus income from his savings. The profit to the neighbourhood is in his being tempted to reinvest his savings in mills and manufactories. How carefully have many lived, how hard have they worked, and how boldly they have sunk their savings in mills, I need not say – you know it as well as I do; though perhaps you may not have reflected so much on the benefits...*

Glossop in 1856 was full of statistics which proved beyond all doubt, to his way of thinking, that mill workers were better fed, longer lived and had a greater quality of life than those who worked in the countryside. Elizabeth had her own passionate ideas about that. There has never been anything to suggest that the friendship between Elizabeth Gaskell and Edmund Potter was anything other than a perfectly proper one, but she based the main character of John Thornton in *North and South* on Edmund Potter and there is no mistaking the smouldering sensuality that lies just beneath the surface.

Although the printing works were in Glossop, Edmund Potter and his eldest son, Crompton (who ran the print works), maintained warehouses in Manchester, which was the international centre for buying and selling cotton. Edmund's warehouse was at 14 Mosley Street, very close to Piccadilly Gardens, an imposing five-storey red-brick warehouse that is today home to Lloyds TSB. Crompton had his father's former warehouse in nearby Charlotte Street, at No.10, close to the Portico Library. Today, appropriately enough, it houses Gibbs Bookshop, which specialises in classical music, antiquarian books and reproductions of 19th-century Ordnance Survey maps.

While very little of Edmund Potter's work has survived, most of Elizabeth Gaskell's has. Cross Street Unitarian Chapel holds an Elizabeth Gaskell Collection and the John Rylands University Archive holds Elizabeth Gaskell manuscripts and first editions. Today Cross Street Unitarian Chapel is built to a modern innovative glass design, quite unlike the one Elizabeth Gaskell would have known. The first Cross Street Chapel was a fine Regency-style pillared and porticoed building; the second, a much more simple and utilitarian building, was destroyed in the Blitz during World War Two. Today the Chapel is working hard to play a positive role in an ever more fragmented community. In addition to holding regular services and caring for the Gaskell items in its possession, the Chapel hosts lunchtime history lectures and coffee mornings, and staff are willing to show visitors round.

Much of Elizabeth Gaskell's work was centred around the Manchester millscapes. The social conditions which the mill workers endured shocked her to the core, just as they shocked Friedrich Engels, who lived not far away in Moss Side.

...women from their doors tossed household slops of every description into the gutter; they ran into the next pool, which overflowed and stagnated. Heaps of ashes were steppingstones, on

The farm that features in Mrs Gaskell's novel Mary Barton *c.1900.* (Manchester Archives & Local Studies, Central Library)

which the passer-by, who cared in the least for cleanliness, took care not to put his foot. Our friends [two factory workers] were not dainty, but even they picked their way, till they got to some steps leading down... into the cellar in which a family of human beings lived.... After the account I have given of the state of the street, no one can be surprised that on going into the cellar inhabited by Davenport, the smell was so foetid as almost to knock the two men down. Quickly recovering themselves, as those inured to such things do, they began to penetrate the thick darkness of the place, and to see three or four children rolling on the damp, nay wet brick floor,

One of the warehouses in Manchester owned by Crompton Potter. This is 10 Charlotte Street, which houses Gibbs Bookshop in the basement.

View of 10 Charlotte Street, Crompton Potter's former warehouse, showing Gibbs Bookshop on the ground floor.

through which the stagnant, filthy moisture of the street oozed up; the fireplace was empty and black; the wife sat on her husband's lair [couch], *and cried in the dank loneliness...*

(Elizabeth Gaskell, *Mary Barton*, Chapter 6, 1848)

Until around 1910 Moss Side was a pretty country area with several farms where Victorian families picnicked on summer afternoons. Mary Barton's farm in Elizabeth's novel *Mary Barton* was based on Pepperhill Farm in Moss Side. Pepperhill Farm survived until 1900 before being demolished. The rural farming community of Moss Side, with its meandering streams and weeping willows, must be one of Manchester's most well hidden secrets. Many Mancunians, even when faced with photographic evidence, cannot bring themselves to believe that Moss Side was ever just that: a small isolated hamlet on the edge of a peat moss. Anyone searching for any trace of 19th-century rural Moss Side will be disappointed, however, because the only places it now exists are in old photographs and descriptions like those in Elizabeth Gaskell's books.

The Taj Mahal of Manchester

THE 'TAJ MAHAL of Manchester' is how the St Francis Monastery on Gorton Lane has been described. It is on a list of the world's most endangered monuments along with the Valley of the Kings in Egypt and the ancient city of Pompeii – unlikely stablemates for an ecclesiastical establishment built during the days of 'Cottonopolis' in a grimy suburb of Manchester, and something that the Franciscan friars could never have foreseen when they first moved to Gorton in 1861.

St Francis of Assisi (1182–1226) and St Clare of Assisi (1194–1253) founded the Franciscan Order. There were a number of orders (both Catholic and Anglican), including the Poor Clares and the Franciscan Order, whose Brothers or friars built Gorton Monastery. The real name of the Franciscan Order is '*ordo fratrum minorum*' meaning 'the order of lesser brothers'.

The Franciscan Order built a chapel school on Gorton Lane. Then in 1862 the Brothers moved into Bankfield, a four-acre site bought for £2,200. They worked hard, tending to the poor and the sick, but still found time to realise their ambitious plans for the monastery. Renowned architect Edward Pugin designed the plans for the church and friary and building work began in 1867. The Brothers, together with local volunteers, built the monastery themselves under the supervision of Brother Dalton. Bricks used in the construction work were made from local clay; and Brother Dalton scoured Manchester looking for unwanted bricks from demolition sites (or from anywhere for that matter) which he could use in the construction work.

The building of the friary was completed in 1867 and the Brothers moved in from Bankswood Cottage. The cottage was then demolished and building of the church continued. The Bishop laid the first stone in 1866. Work was slow and laborious. In 1871 an appeal had to be made for extra public funding. The church was sufficiently complete by 1872 for it to be opened. It was 184ft (56m) long, 98ft (29.6m) wide and 100ft (30.3m) high. The

Gorton Monastery, 1915.
(Manchester Archives &
Local Studies, Central
Library)

finished church had red bricks, with blue brick and stone dressings and slate
roofs. It included a sanctuary, side chapels, a nave and aisles, divided by six
arches. 'Pointed arched windows and rose windows, a particular feature of
Gothic architecture, allow natural light to cascade throughout the church...'
A pale green bell turret perched on top of a narrow steeple. *The Catholic
Times* trumpeted that the structure was '...a triumph of Catholic
architecture'.

In 1882 the wooden floors of the monastery, which had been warped by
the damp atmosphere in Gorton, were replaced with Irish limestone tiles.
Gifts of a stained-glass altar window, Lady Chapel, Sanctuary Lamp,
wrought-iron communion railing, a font and a pulpit were gratefully received
by the monastery and the church was finally completed in 1885 when the
high altar was installed. The '...high altar was designed by Peter Paul Pugin
and carved out of Bath stone... the Brothers enterprisingly set up a special
workshop to carve the stone in the grounds of the Friary...'.

On clear mornings the rays of the rising sun shine through the upper rows
of diametrically opposite windows, the sparkling glass giving the church a
golden halo which transcends the grey confines of its industrial surroundings
to give the building an almost ethereal air.

The monastery remains an unusually fine example of 'high Victorian

Gothic architecture', although it is now disused and badly in need of restoration. The front façade of the friary was demolished in the 1970s and the Brothers moved out after over a century of caring for the spiritual welfare of Gorton and leaving behind them a unique creation which had been lovingly sculpted by the bare hands of their forefathers. The final mass was held in 1989. Twelve statues of the saints, rescued from the nave, are held in storage by Manchester City Council. In spite of the problems , however, the towering façade of the church with its tiny bell tower still has the power to impress and it remains an enigmatic landmark within Manchester millscapes.

The complete regeneration scheme, known as 'The Angels', includes a five-phase scheme over five years. When complete it will include:

The Pugin Centre (Phase I): restoration and re-opening of St Francis Church and Friary (Gorton Monastery) as a Cultural Heritage, Exhibition and Enterprise Centre.

The Angels Healthy Living Centre/Medical Services (Phase II): creation of a new wing where the original Friary was demolished to house a Medical Centre, Pharmacy, and Healthy Living Centre facility.

The Angels Healthy Living Centre/Community Services (Phase III): creation of a second, contemporary courtyard to provide dedicated community services & an integrated hub of health provision on one site.

The Angels Traditional Skills Workshops, Learning & Invention Centre (Phase IV): former garage premises will become traditional skills workshops offering training in stonemasonry, carving and sculpture as well as stained-glass restoration and traditional furniture making.

The Angels Community Village (Phase V): a mixed use development of:

- The Manchester School of Osteopaths
- United Co-op Convenience Store
- Greater Manchester Play Resource Unit (Grumpy)
- The 'Smart Risk' Lifeskills Centre & Crucial Crew
- JVCo Managed Workspace
- A Neighbourhood Nursery
- St John Ambulance

(restoration and regeneration details courtesy of The Monastery Trust of St Francis and Gorton website http://www.gortonmonastery.co.uk)

Hanging Bridge and Hanging Ditch

ONE OF THE most enduring mysteries of Manchester was the legend of its lost bridge. For around 200 years the only clue to the existence of the bridge was in the name Hanging Bridge. The bridge supposedly derived its name from the river or stream that it crossed, known as Hanging Ditch; though some thought the name came from the fact that it had been a rope bridge strung across the river like those in remote jungle areas.

The mystery was solved during demolition work in the 1880s when astonished labourers found part of the arch of a bridge several feet below ground. The City Surveyors department was called in and they supervised a careful excavation. Slowly a double-arch stone bridge began to emerge. The bridge was 36 yards (just over 30m) long and 3 yards (2.75m) wide. It had therefore not been merely a hanging rope bridge, but a solid well-built structure capable of carrying a decent volume of traffic.

Part of the bridge, however, was of an earlier date than the rest, including the buttress of the southern arch, and there were indications that this might have been the foundation of a draw-bridge which could have given substance to the legend of a hanging bridge. In 1937 it was surmised that there was an open space at the Cateaton Street end of the bridge (close to the present positions of Sinclair's Oyster Bar and the Old Wellington Inn) where executions took place – hence the name Hanging Bridge. The most likely explanation though is of a far more natural origin, which involves another of Manchester's legends: that of its lost rivers.

There are historical references to the *Hengand Brigge* in 1343. It crossed a deep ditch or fosse through which a swift flowing stream descended from the

Hanging Bridge rediscovered, 1890. (Manchester Archives & Local Studies, Central Library)

River Irk to the River Irwell. By the time it reached the Irwell the ditch was 120ft (37m) wide and 40ft (12.3m) deep. This stream is considered by many to have been the lost River Dene from which Deansgate (Denes Gate) takes its name. The prefix 'hen-' is normally an Old English reference to wild birds such as moorhens and waterhens; while the suffix '-gan' derives from a Welsh word for 'situated between two hills'.

In 1343 Manchester was little more than a village surrounded by open countryside and moorland across which numerous rivers and streams flowed. Where the Cathedral stands today there was a small parish church nestling on the sandstone outcrop that had been a centre of settlement since Celtic times. A bridge across the rushing stream deep in its valley linked the church to the heart of mediaeval Manchester. Hanging Bridge is mentioned in the records of the Court Leet (the local magistrates of the time) and there is a reference that '...dyvers persons drove oxen across it and through the grave yard for a short cut...'

Most of the bridge found in the 1880s dates from the 15th century, when it must have been rebuilt using part of the foundations of the earlier bridge. This may have been occasioned by the 10th-century parish church of St Mary being granted Collegiate Church status in 1421 and becoming an important ecclesiastical establishment. In 1600 the Hanging Ditch was condemned as being an open sewer and in 1682 it disappears from the records. It is known that by 1800, as the population of Manchester was exploding with the coming of 'Cottonopolis', the ditch had been culverted and the Hanging Bridge built over; and in 1772 *Raffald's Directory* recorded that nine houses were built along the line of the bridge. It is likely that the Hanging Bridge was buried and covered over in the first phase of proper town planning during the 1770s. Out of sight and out of mind the bridge passed into legend until its accidental rediscovery nearly a century later.

In April 1900 a letter written to the *Manchester Guardian* added a touch of mystery to Hanging Bridge:

...I was shown a door in Hanging Bridge Hotel cellar where the arches could be seen and a door made up... it was the entrance to an underground passage under the Irwell, possibly to Ordsall Hall... the owner had not traversed the passage himself, but the previous owner had, but had to turn back because of bad smells...

Things took a sinister turn in the *Manchester Notes and Queries* for
November 1901:

> *...when the licensed house at the Cathedral end of Hanging Bridge
> was rebuilt, a tunnel was found with five or six skeletons with
> fragments of clothing and copper coin with Latin inscription...*

This was said to be copper coinage, probably from the reign of Queen Mary
Tudor and her husband, King Philip II of Spain (1553–8).

H.T. Crofton, a contributor to the Lancashire and Cheshire Antiquarian
Society, noted that:

> *...peculiar stonework on the middle pier indicates a chapel could
> have been here, supported by a flying buttress on the Irwell-west
> side. Masonry at the north end was very massive indeed, and the
> building of this north end also projected considerably beyond the
> arches...*

This is interesting, especially in the light of Tudor traveller and writer, John
Leland, who writes of Manchester in his *Itinerary* of 1540, and says '...there
be divers stone bridges... but the best of three arches is over Irwel... on this
bridge is a praty little chapel [a pretty little chantry chapel which later became
a prison]...'

Although it was obvious that the rushing stream had long since dried up,
it would perhaps have been more appropriate if the Hanging Ditch and
Hanging Bridge could have remained an open feature; a memory of the
mediaeval village where the textile industry of the 19th century had its roots.
However this was not to be. Most of Hanging Ditch had been culverted and
built over. The Corn and Produce Exchange, now known as the Triangle
shopping complex, stands along the length of the ditch and the name is
commemorated in the short stretch of pedestrianised street running from

*The excavation of
Hanging Bridge, 1892.
(Manchester Archives &
Local Studies, Central
Library)*

Corporation Street to Cateaton Street (which
begins where the Old Wellington Inn presently
stands).

Hanging Bridge has survived, although not
easily visible from the outside as it is still mostly
hidden by buildings. The best things are often
discovered by accident and the Hanging Bridge
proved to be no exception. Taking shelter from a
bitter north-east wind the writer of this book
decided to go in search of hot coffee from the

Mediaeval Hanging Bridge, built of stone near Manchester Cathedral. Now partly hidden by modern buildings, it forms part of a coffee shop.

refectory in the basement of the Cathedral shop and information centre. There, forming one side of the refectory, was the Hanging Bridge.

The stonework of the Bridge has been fully restored and the floor has been tiled. Tables and chairs have been placed under the northern arch looking through French windows along a short grassy length of the former ditch. Alternatively, patrons can sit up on a higher level and look down the length of the Bridge. The wood and tiles of the modern coffee bar complement the old mediaeval stone arches quite naturally.

It is a strange feeling to sit in the bed of a lost river beneath the Hanging Bridge, drinking some of the best cappuccino to be had in Manchester, and reflecting that no doubt even the mediaeval ox drivers would have been impressed by the size and quality of the pastries and baguettes on offer with the coffee. It is an unusual and charming way of preserving such an integral part of the city's history.

Heaton Hall and Boggart Hole Clough

HEATON HALL was originally built by the Egerton family during the late 1600s. Sir Thomas Egerton inherited the hall in 1756. He was a wealthy man whose money came from owning the mineral rights on his estates. In 1772 he married an heiress, Eleanor Assheton, and commissioned James Wyatt, an architect of some renown, to design and rebuild the house. Some of Wyatt's interior work was inspired by Robert Adam. The plasterwork was done by Joseph Rose II of York, while the furniture and the mahogany doors came from Gillow of Lancaster. Italian artist, Biagio Rebecca, painted most of the decorative work and pictures, as well as the Pompeiian Cupola Room. In 1820 Lewis Wyatt remodelled the library and added the Orangery. The hall today is a listed Grade I building because of the excellence of its neo-classical design.

Guests as diverse as the Duke of Wellington and the actress Fanny Kemble, Disraeli and Tom Thumb (Charles Stratton [1838–83] an American dwarf just 31in high who was known as General Tom Thumb), stayed at Heaton Hall when visiting Manchester. Heaton Park, the grounds in which the hall stands, covers 640 acres, making it Manchester's largest park. In the early 19th century the well-known Heaton Park Races were run on the site of the lake. The large boating lake is fronted by the façade of Manchester's first Town Hall, which was in King Street and was demolished in 1912. It is described as 'an architectural copy of the Greek Erechtheion in Athens'.

Heaton Park was used during World War One for billeting and training soldiers near Hollows Lane and there was a mock-up of the infamous battlefield trenches of France. This now lies under a pitch and putt golf course. There was also a hospital in a large house at the top of nearby Bowker

Heaton Hall, 1972.
(Manchester Archives &
Local Studies, Central
Library)

Vale during World War One. During this period a musician with a hurdy-gurdy or a barrel organ would come and play at the bottom of Hollows Lane on summer evenings.

Today the Park has 'swan boats' on the boating lake. A huge rock set in a field close by is known as the Papal Monument, and there is also a tram museum. Old tram tracks are still visible in the Park. The Orangery at the hall has been transformed into a restaurant and conference centre; and a farm centre has been established where Highland cattle, little black faced Soay sheep, peacocks and waterfowl are bred.

Boggart Hole Clough, near the hall, is one of Manchester's lesser known parks; a local 'beauty spot' with dramatic landscape, woodlands and water. It was supposed to be haunted in more peaceful times by a green boggart. One story tells of a farm at the head of the Clough near White Moss. The farmer and his family of several children were plagued by a boggart, 'an unquiet spirit that manifested itself in a small shrill voice like a baby's penny trumpet...' At first the boggart was fairly harmless, but then one of the sons of the house poked fun at it. The boggart took great exception to this and things started to get a bit heavy with injuries being inflicted. Finally the boggart tried to suffocate one of the farmer's children in bed. The farmer had had enough. He packed up his family and moved to new premises.

A later legend, however, paints a kinder picture of the boggart. 'Tread softly,' wrote this story teller, 'for... Boggart Clough, and see in yonder dark corners, and beneath projecting mossy stones, where the dusky sullen cave yawns before you... there lurks a strange elf, the sly and mischievous boggart.' Young men would try to win the love of a particular girl by 'going into the Clough for three grains of St John's fernseed in which the boggart frolicked...'

Boggart Hole Clough is still wooded countryside, though today Booth Hall Children's Hospital stands opposite; but this particular boggart does not seem to have cared much for the march of progress and it is many years now since it was either seen or heard.

In a letter to the *Manchester Guardian* in October 1874 a writer offered a different explanation:

> *...Near here* [Valentine's Brow] *and looking up the brook there was a mound like a tumulus. This was called Mal's grave. Just above that, where the ground rises to a natural elevation of some 15 feet or so, is a little plateau, about 50 feet by 25 feet in its widest part. This is called Mal's garden. The grave has gone but the garden will remain...*

First Town Hall portico façade, Heaton Hall, 1972. (Manchester Archives & Local Studies, Central Library)

Colour changes – Manchester's hidden textile industry

UNTIL THE early 19th century the places known today as the northern suburbs within Manchester city boundaries were pretty little villages nestling in the Lancashire countryside. Since mediaeval times in these villages there had been cottage industries of dyeing and there was a tradition of linen weaving, washing and bleaching in the Moston and Newton Heath areas which continued even after mechanisation and the discovery of artificial aniline dyes in the 1850s.

Bleaching and dyeing are the important finishing processes of manufacturing cotton fabrics and the villages of Harpurhey, Crumpsall, Blackley, Moston and Collyhurst became centres for the dyeing and bleaching industries because they were 'too far off and too dry for cotton mills...' Further south the little cluster of Miles Platting, Clayton and Newton Heath also had chemical and dye works.

Woven cotton's natural colour is a sort of creamy off-white. A good bright white was much prized and it is best to bleach textiles before dyeing to ensure a good even spread of colour.

The methods of bleaching before mechanisation were quite lengthy and could take a whole summer. Cloth was soaked in a lye (a liquid leached from wood ash) and then for a further week in a potash lye; a process known as 'bucking'.

It was then washed and placed under pressure in wooden barrels of buttermilk for another week. Afterwards the cloth was spread out on the grass of a bleach field or on a frame supported by tenter posts, to dry and bleach in the sunshine (crofting). Tenter posts still exist in the countryside to the north of Manchester.

When it was dry the cloth would then be soaked in sour milk for several days, washed and crofted again. This whole process was repeated several times until the cloth had acquired the requisite degree of whiteness. While the cloth was spread out drying it was vulnerable to theft. This crime was known as croft breaking, and the penalty for stealing cloth in this way was severe. Offenders were usually sentenced to death, and in 1798 a lad from Newton Heath was executed for stealing from a local bleaching croft.

Blackley, on the edge of which stands Heaton Hall, was originally owned by the Byron family, ancestors of the colourful romantic 19th-century poet Lord Byron. Linen weaving had been a cottage industry since the 16th century when French immigrants escaping religious persecution had settled in the area. Heaton Mills were built for the dyeing and printing of textiles close to the remains of a weir built to supply a water-driven corn mill near Hollow Lane.

Collyhurst, famed in the early 1800s for growing a 7ft 8in (2.3m) long cucumber in its local tea gardens (which sadly no longer exist), expanded rapidly during the latter part of the 19th century. Collyhurst Dye Works stood near Dalton Street and there were three or four other dye works on the banks of the River Irk and a cotton worsted dye works on Crampton's Lane in Hendham Vale.

In 1850 Joseph Johnson wrote of '...the pretty village of Crumpsall...' and another contemporary writer noted that '...Crumpsall was a pleasant country village unspoilt by industry and surrounded by fields in which wild flowers grow in profusion...' The village was on the edge of the dyeing and bleaching industries but 'Cottonopolis' was a demanding mistress. Farmland disappeared, along with the '...wild flowers which grow in profusion...', the salmon in the River Irk, and '...the brook in which watercress grew...' Later Crumpsall became home to ICI.

There had been a cottage industry of linen weaving and bleaching since the 16th century in neighbouring Newton Heath as well as in Moston. There was a silk mill in Newton Heath and this mill collaborated with the Monsall Dye Works to produce sarsnet, a soft silk fabric used for ribbons. Dye works sprang up along the banks of the Rochdale Canal and the nearby River Medlock.

Before the discovery of artificial or aniline dyes during the 19th century, dyeing was done by natural methods using the flowers, berries, leaves, bark and roots of plants and herbs.

Common sources for natural dyes include:

red:	madder (root); meadowsweet (root)
yellow:	weld; bog myrtle; marsh marigold; golden rod
blue:	woad (leaves); elder (berries); cornflower
green:	nettles (roots, stalk, leaves); lily of the valley; bracken (buds)
purple:	deadly nightshade; elder (berries); dandelion (root)
brown:	blackthorn; larch (needles); onion (skins)
black:	blackberry (shoots); alder (bark); oak (bark/acorns); water lily (root)

Manchester became justly famous in this little-known area of the textile industry.

Large supplies of fairly pure, soft water are required for... dyeing and printing; hence the banks of the rivers... Medlock, Irk... and Irwell... are well lined with works belonging to that group...
(L.S. Wood, and A. Wilmore, *The Romance of the Cotton Industry in England*, OUP.)

One of the incentives for England to produce its own cottons was the popularity of the beautifully dyed muslins and chintzes which were being imported from India. English manufacturers were faced with the problems of reproducing the scarlets and indigoes, deep purples and greens of the Indian prints. In the early days of cotton production they were frustrated because the madder reds used in their dyeing processes were extremely prone to running.

Harpurhey, to the north east of Cheetham and three or four miles from the city centre, came to prominence in the 19th century when the Andrew family bought the whole of the Harpurhey lands in 1812. The family worked in the dyeing trade and their new dye works, which stood near Moss Brook, became very successful in the production of Turkey Red, a new colour-fast red dye which did not run like the old madder reds. They then went on to develop a new pale lilac print. The road on which their dye works stood was named Turkey Red Lane in honour of their new achievement.

Harpurhey was described by a 19th-century writer:

It was very pretty countryside close to Hendham Vale where the River Irk, then a clear stream full of fish, ran through woodlands full of wild hyacinths and meadows of daffodils and primroses...

This Harpurhey is no longer recognisable but Turkey Red Lane has survived.

Although lilac was a pretty shade of colour, the colours of mauve and deep purple as they are known today did not then exist. However, in 1855, William Perkin, who was a student at the Royal College of Chemistry, inadvertently produced the colour mauve during experiments. As Perkin began to realise the importance of his discovery he applied for a patent which was granted:

> *Letters patent (No. 1984) to William Henry Perkin... for the invention of producing a new colouring matter for dyeing silk, cotton etc. with a lilac or purple colour... Creator Perkin, Professor William Henry*
> *Description Provisional specification of the method for producing Perkins synthetic dye, as presented to the Office of the Commissioners of Patents.*
> *Patent sealed 20th February 1857. Date Created 26th August 1856*

This discovery revolutionised the dyeing industry and Manchester was quick to take advantage. Shortly afterwards purple was successfully produced and one of the earliest purple cotton dresses was manufactured in Manchester in around 1857. The dress has survived and is on display at Quarry Bank Mill, about two miles from Manchester Airport.

A Manchester waterway polluted by the mills and dye works standing along its banks. (Manchester Archives & Local Studies, Central Library)

Hidden Gem

UNTIL THE Act of Religious Toleration was passed in 1791 Catholic worship had been forbidden since the days of Queen Mary Tudor (1553–8). Her father, Henry VIII, had broken with Rome and the Pope in his desperate bid to divorce her mother, Catherine of Aragon, so that he could marry Anne Boleyn. Her half-brother, Edward VI, retained their father's Protestant religion, but when Edward died prematurely, aged only 15, Mary ascended the throne and returned England to Catholic worship with a vengeance. Those who opposed her were likely to find themselves burnt at the stake. She married King Philip II of Spain (her mother's homeland) and vowed that she would found a new Catholic dynasty of monarchs. In the event Mary died childless and the last of the Tudor siblings, Elizabeth I, the daughter of Anne Boleyn, ensured that England would remain Protestant and that never again would a Catholic monarch sit on the throne.

The backlash against the Catholics was considerable. Mary's determination to burn heretics (those who did not believe in the Catholic doctrine) earned her the nickname of Bloody Mary and provoked a dislike of all things Catholic among many of the English people. Those whose families had worshipped the 'old religion' for centuries continued to do so, but under conditions of the utmost secrecy. They were not allowed to build churches, publicly worship in their faith, or hold services or mass. The penalties for being found out were harsh in the extreme.

As time passed attitudes mellowed and there was a call for people to be allowed to worship according to their conscience. When the Act of Religious Toleration was finally passed Catholics were free to practise their religion and ways of worship openly. Relieved and jubilant, the members of England's Catholic community rejoiced and began building Catholic churches. It is against this backdrop of history that St Mary's, the 'hidden gem', was built in 1792, making it the '…oldest post-Reformation Catholic church founded as a church in any major centre of population in England…'

St Mary's was built between Deansgate and Albert Square; at that time an area of great poverty where destitution and prostitution were common. The church stood on Mulberry Street which, until a few years beforehand, had been meadow land and pasture, but was now covered by cheap shanty housing for those coming in off the land to work in the rapidly expanding millscapes. Mulberry Street is now a little back street, hidden from sight by the buildings of Deansgate, John Dalton Street, Albert Square and Brazennose Street. St Mary's graveyard is still in situ but has not been in use for a long time and most of it will be hidden under modern buildings.

St Mary's was painted in a winter setting by L.S. Lowry in 1962. He called it *The Hidden Gem in the Snow* and he captured the essence of the hidden church, snuggled in its back street yet still a focus for the community. The church is very proud of its Adams Stations of the Cross which are nationally important works of art. They are savagely colourful and impressive, ranged along the side walls of the church. Sir Philip Dowson, President of the Royal Academy of Art, said of them in 1995 '...is it not wonderful, at the end of this century, that our minds are being raised by the greatest of modern art to our Lord's saving passion...'

The interior of St Mary's is clean and white and colourful with brown/white marble support pillars. The central dome has eight pairs of beautiful stained-glass windows with Latin inscriptions. Candles of remembrance burn in the church, flickering brightly. There is a feeling of great peace. People come to pray, to admire the works of art, to wander, or simply to escape from the frantic 21st-century materialistic world outside for a few minutes. One does not need to be a Catholic to appreciate that St Mary's is a quiet and welcoming oasis for those of all faiths or none.

The 'Hidden Gem' on Mulberry Street, 1958. (Manchester Archives & Local Studies, Central Library)

Hulme Hall

HULME HALL Road is not an area where one cares to be alone, even in broad daylight with a fitful sun shining through the clouds. It is easy to understand why those in the dingy workshops and garages which squat in the archways beneath the railway line look at strangers with caution and regard those who wish to wander there out of choice as perhaps a sandwich short of a picnic. There is a large cobbled area in front of the landward side of the railway arches with what look like disused railway lines running across. These are in fact the remains of a 'horse wagon way' from pre-motorised days when goods were transported in horse-drawn carts to and from the banks of the Irwell and the nearby Bridgewater Canal to their destination.

Hulme Hall Road passes beneath the railway arches and ends at a bridge across the Irwell to Woden Street (named after the Danish god of thunder), which leads to Ordsall Lane. On the other side of the bridge, a towpath, lit by mock Victorian lamps, and named Ordsall Lane Walk, Irwell, leads along the north-west bank of the river. On either side of the bridge on the railway side a grassy bank supports the ground over which the railway arches run. Originally they carried the Cheshire Lines across Hulme; today it is the Metrolink branch line to Eccles, next stop Pomona Docks. Beneath the bank to the left is a flat grassy area and a footpath with railings and the same mock Victorian lamps as across the river. This was the site of Hulme Hall, a mediaeval manor where hidden treasure is said to lie buried.

A more unromantic setting for such a place would be hard to imagine. Mental gymnastics are required to make the leap from modern industrial detritus to days of old when knights were bold. Hulme used to be romantic enough. Originally a small farming settlement by the river in the days of the Vikings, it had grown into a village by the 18th century with its own manor house, Hulme Hall, a picturesque black and white timbered building standing on the banks of the Irwell. The hall was demolished in 1845; too early for there to have been any photographs of it; but there is an etching of 1833 showing a gabled and dilapidated Tudor house standing forlornly downstream from the encroaching millscapes.

Like all old houses of a certain age the hall was said to be haunted, but these were no ordinary ghosts. A 19th-century writer described them in sinister fashion as 'unearthly guardians, demon charms' who prowled the grounds guarding the secret location of buried treasure. During the Civil War (1640–9) the Lady Dowager Prestwich encouraged her son, Sir Thomas Prestwich, whose family had owned Hulme Hall since the early 1300s, to part with large sums of money to the Royalist cause (although Manchester's sympathies lay with the Roundheads) and promised that she would repay him with treasure which she had buried in the grounds of the hall so that Cromwell's men should not find it.

The horse wagon way on Hulme Hall Road, 1973. (Manchester Archives & Local Studies, Central Library)

According to legend, the Lady Dowager had given her treasure extra protection by means of secret magic spells which she cast by the riverside when the moon was full. However, before she could tell Sir Thomas of its whereabouts she was seized by a mysterious illness which struck her dumb and left her paralysed. The doctors could do nothing for her and she died without being able to reveal her secret to anyone.

In victory the Parliamentarians were neither generous nor forgiving and vented their anger on Sir Thomas for supporting the king. He was heavily fined and part of his estates were confiscated. In despair Sir Thomas spent the rest of his life searching in vain for the treasure. He never discovered where it lay hidden and he died in great poverty. He mortgaged the hall to Nicholas Mosley of Ancoats, who bought it outright in 1673. Later the hall became the property of the Bland family and it was the house in which Lady Ann Bland, who built St Ann's Church in St Ann's Square, spent her childhood. In 1764 the Hall was purchased by the Duke of Bridgewater.

The Duke of Bridgewater was not much interested in Hulme Hall itself. It lay close to the newly completed Bridgewater Canal and doubtless the Duke bought the place as an investment in land which might later sell for a good price. However, during the 18th and early 19th century tales of the buried treasure had become well known and unscrupulous fortune tellers would cheat the unwary out of their money by claiming to know where the treasure lay. Whether the Duke knew of these tales is not clear, but he didn't seem to make much effort to deter hopeful 'get-rich-quick punters' from digging on his land. No one ever found anything, but still the stories persisted.

By 1845 Hulme Hall was in a dilapidated condition and it was demolished to make way for the railway. Just before demolition several panels of grotesque wooden figures were removed from the hall and taken to Worsley

The site of Hulme Hall, where 'unearthly demons' are said to guard buried treasure.

Hall. Some said that these were likenesses of the 'demon charms' that the Lady Dowager had set to guard her treasure and that with their departure the treasure would be found; but despite the demolition and subsequent building work the treasure remained undiscovered.

Although it is surrounded by industrial units, workshops, tower blocks, waste ground and half built shells of 'regeneration', the spot where Hulme Hall stood beside the river remains remarkably peaceful. The former rural idyll of Hulme, where 'the white bells of Galatea's lovely convolvulus' bloomed in summer, seems closer here.

Despite all that modern technology has to offer the treasure has not been found to this day and it seems that the 'unearthly guardians' have done their job well. Perhaps there never was any treasure; or perhaps it was not treasure of the conventional sort; but stories of the hidden treasure persisted for over 200 years and there is always a grain of truth in folklore. On nights when a hunter's moon rides high above scudding clouds and the river glides past, silent and sparkling in the moonlight, it is not hard to imagine the old Lady Dowager standing with her arms raised, invoking forces of power we can only guess at, entreating them to guard her treasure against all comers for all time; and maybe, just maybe, she succeeded.

Cheetham, Strangeways and the Jewish Museum

MANCHESTER has had a Jewish community of some size for the last 200 years. Jewish cotton merchants first arrived in Manchester during the early 19th century, attracted by the explosion in cotton manufacturing and cotton goods production caused by the Industrial Revolution. The millscapes were a grim place to live. Cheetham was a pretty country village less than a mile distant from the commercial centre and seemed an ideal place for the Jewish merchants to settle. They congregated in the area now known as Cheetham Hill.

Once famed for its archers and a favourite haunt of the highwayman Dick Turpin, Cheetham is rather better known today for Boddingtons brewery and the notorious Strangeways prison. During the first part of the 19th century Cheetham Hill was a pleasant and genteel place in which to live. As late as 1850 there were tea gardens in Cheetwood Village (part of Cheetham) where the air was 'sweet with the perfume of roses, pinks, carnations, mignonette... in midsummer the smell of new mown hay... in the orchards, currant and gooseberry trees... pear and apple trees...'

However, during the latter half of the 19th century, things began to change. The main cause was the demand for housing from people coming to work in the ever-expanding millscapes. Hundreds of small terraced houses were built on what had been meadow land. A journalist of the time wrote that the '...open countryside of the 1820s was a solid mass of bricks and mortar by the 1870s...'

After the 1860s Cheetham was gradually overwhelmed by urbanisation but the Jewish people were relatively happy and settled within their own community and they stayed. As well as their merchanting expertise their tailoring skills were much in demand and Cheetham suited them well.

R.W. Procter, in his *Memorials of Manchester Streets*, paints a very different picture of the Strangeways area before industrialisation:

> *...the ponds adjoining Strangeways Hall were well stocked with choice fish and offered seasonable amusements to anglers... young bathers, sliders, skaters here abounded... in summer narrow escapes from drowning, and in winter fatal disasters upon treacherous ice were of frequent occurrence... one night, in the darkness of winter, the passers-by heard shrieking sounds; but the wind being high and whistling through the scattered trees in the neighbouring clough, no notice was taken. In the morning, however, an elderly dame was discovered in the water... nearly half a century she had been known as a muffin-crier thereabouts, and wandering from the pathway had sunk into the pond...*

Several synagogues were built in Cheetham to cater for the religious needs of the community. These included the Great Synagogue, built in 1858 and demolished in 1986; the Reform Synagogue, built in 1858 and destroyed during the Blitz in 1941; and the Spanish and Portuguese Synagogue, built in 1874, which now houses the only Jewish Museum in Britain. Jews who lived in Spain or Portugal are known as Sephardi and were expelled from those countries during the Spanish Inquisition of the 15th century. Their traditions, customs and style of service, if not their religious beliefs, differ from those of the Ashkenazi Jews of Eastern and Central Europe.

The Spanish and Portuguese Synagogue was built on a 'Saracenic' design, by Edward Salomons, according to Sephardi traditions which are reflected in the decorative frontage and the Moorish arches. It was the custom for roofs to be fashioned from freshly cut branches and open to the sky; but though this worked in the warmer, drier Iberian climate it was impractical for Manchester, so instead '...a rolling roof, a light roof resting on tracks...' was used.

During the latter part of the 20th century there was a population shift. Today Cheetham has a larger Asian population. Consequently the Spanish and Portuguese Synagogue's role declined and the last service was held there in 1982. Much internal restoration work was done and in 1984 the Synagogue re-opened as the Jewish Museum. Like other synagogues it faces east to Jerusalem with the 'ark' at the western end. The beautiful stained-glass windows, each depicting a scene from the Bible, and the cast-iron fitments remain. The ark is still a prominent feature. This is the satin-lined cupboard where the sacred Torah scrolls (on which the five books of the Old Testament are hand-written) are kept. These are read in turn throughout each year. Above the ark burns an everlasting light to commemorate the lamp kept burning in the Temple of Jerusalem.

The pews line either side of the Synagogue at right angles to the ark

The Jewish Museum on Cheetham Hill Road, 1975. (Manchester Archives & Local Studies, Central Library)

and the Torah. Males and females are seated separately in Orthodox synagogues and the Ladies Gallery runs round at first-floor level directly above the pews for the men. The seating has been removed and an exhibition gallery created which includes Jewish archive items, pictures and arts; as well as a kitchen, with a dining table set specially for the Sabbath, and a waterproof garment makers workshop.

The Jewish Museum welcomes visitors but they still observe the Jewish Sabbath from sunset on Friday evening to nightfall on Saturday, so the Museum is generally closed at those times. It is a unique museum and its importance was recognised by a visit from the Queen in 2003.

Other Jewish institutions in Cheetham included a Jewish School on Torah Street, the Talmud Torah (talmud – teaching; torah – law), now a storage warehouse; the Manchester Jews School and the well-known Nathan Hope's Cloth Caps factory on Derby Street in the shadow of Strangeways gaol. The factory started production in the 1850s when cloth caps were very popular. A mostly Jewish workforce was employed under stringent conditions. If a worker broke a needle it had to be paid for from their wages. Opposite Nathan Hope's factory lay the first Marks & Spencer warehouse.

In 1884 Michael Marks had opened a penny bazaar stall at Kirkgate Market in Leeds. He moved to Cheetham Hill Road in 1893, living and working at No.20. Legend says that Mr Marks's slogan was 'don't ask the price, it's a penny' because he did not know enough English to barter. The following year he went into partnership with Tom Spencer and the world-famous company of Marks & Spencer was born. They opened their first warehouse and new head office on Derby Street in 1901; and together they became a household name for quality clothing at affordable prices.

A Gothic Tribute

AS ONE woman's memorial to her husband it has to rank among the most impressive of all time. The John Rylands Library is said to be '...the finest example of neo-Gothic architecture in Europe...' It is built of grey and rose pink Cumbrian sandstone with panelling and fittings of Polish oak. The ceilings are decorated with white moulded plasterwork while the bronze light fittings, radiator grilles and other metal work are Art Nouveau. The building was the work of Basil Champneys, who also designed Mansfield College in Oxford, and it took nine years to complete.

The Library stands discreetly on Deansgate, seemingly understated, adjacent to the Manchester Evening News headquarters, on the corner of the appropriately named Spinningfield. The Deansgate area once had a reputation for unsavoury pubs and 'ladies of the night', but that is all in the past. Opposite the John Rylands Library is a shop which sells bibles of every religious type and size. Further down towards the Cathedral on the same side as the John Rylands Library establishments include Kendal Milne (Manchester's answer to Harrods) and a large tapas bar, while on the opposite side there is Whittards, which sells a wide range of coffees and teas for the connoisseur, and Waterstone's bookshop.

There are several branches of Waterstone's in Manchester but this is the big one. Three floors of books on every subject under the sun. On the top floor, looking down Deansgate towards the John Rylands Library, is a coffee shop where customers can browse through books of their choice, drinking cappuccino or an impossibly large hot chocolate full of cream and marshmallows while munching on a delightful variety of home-made cookies.

John Rylands died in 1888. Although married three times he had no surviving children and his fortune passed to his widow, Enriqueta. He had been '...Manchester's most successful cotton magnate and one of the

wealthiest self-made Englishmen of his day...' Rylands's merchanting warehouse, a plain white five-storey building which stood out from the surrounding rather more decorative grey stone warehouses, still stands on the corner of Piccadilly Gardens and Tib Street, and today houses Debenhams department store. Enriqueta had adored her husband and she wanted to establish something beautiful and long-lasting, of which he would have been proud, and which would ensure that his name was not forgotten by future generations.

The Library cost £500,000 to build and opened on New Year's Day 1900. A new institution on a new day in a new month in a new year in a new century. Enriqueta was an intelligent woman and she realised that if her Library was to be considered serious and academic and stand the test of time its collections had to reflect those aims and it was not going to be cheap. Her only stipulation was that the collections should have a bias towards Nonconformist theology. In 1892 she purchased 43,000 volumes for £210,000 from the 2nd Earl Spencer. This was followed in 1901 by 6,000 manuscripts from the Bibliotheca Lindesiana (amassed by the 25th and 26th Earls of Crawford) at a cost of £155,000. When she died in 1908 she bequeathed endowments to the Library so that by the 1920s

The interior of the John Rylands Library, 1950. (Manchester Archives & Local Studies, Central Library)

180,000 additional books and 3,000 manuscripts had been added to the collections. Consequently a new extension had to be built at the rear of the Library.

There are marble statues in the foyer by John Cassidy called 'Theology directing the labours of Science and Art' which sum up Mrs Rylands's objectives for her library. The main staircase is curving and vaulted and more in keeping with some splendid mediaeval castle than with a 19th-century library on Deansgate. The danger is that, in admiring the vaulted ceilings and the fluted architecture and the lantern, people will miss their step.

The Reading Room is built at first-floor level to minimise traffic noise. At each end is a huge stained-glass window. The northern one depicts Moses, Isaiah and other biblical figures through history; while the southern one features Aristotle, Beethoven, Dante and Michaelangelo. There is an upper gallery and on the outer edges there are 20 stone statues representing the fields of religion, literature, science and printing, which include John Wesley, Shakespeare, Sir Isaac Newton and William Caxton. A central aisle runs the length of the Reading Room and there are bookcases and study areas in side alcoves. At the far end is John Cassidy's marble statue of John Rylands, gazing down the room towards the issue desk, in front of which stands Cassidy's marble statue of his wife Enriqueta; a loving couple, immortalised in marble, facing each other through eternity, as they preside over one of Manchester's lesser known but glittering jewels.

Today the Library collections are priceless. They include 4,000 'incunabula' (books printed before 1501), three quarters of which date from before 1480; a copy of the Gutenberg Bible; the St Christopher Woodcut of 1423 (Europe's oldest surviving dateable example of printing); Caxton's *Canterbury Tales*; Wynkyn de Worde's *Morte d'Arthur* of 1498; Shakespeare texts; most major 19th-century English writers; bibles in almost every language; Sir Isaac Newton's *Principia Mathematica*; illustrated books on birds and flowers; herbals; Chinese and Japanese texts; the French Revolution; the English Civil War; Jewish literature; archives of local families and early cotton companies; scientific papers of John Dalton (a Manchester teacher, who was the first to describe colour blindness, and a chemist renowned for his work on atomic theory) and Sir Bernard Lovell who was responsible for the Jodrell Bank radio telescope. One of the saddest items is the death and injury compensation book for the Peterloo Massacre of 1819.

Archive storage of many of these items is in huge subterranean 'walk-in' safes which are locked every night. Wandering the dimly lit corridors between the safes and walking into the safes is an eerie experience. So much history is contained in this silent half-light that the air is full of echoes. The archives are not open to the public but there are exhibition cases in the main Reading Room and there is an Exhibition Hall where various of the Library's treasures are displayed in turn. There are regular guided tours of the library and enquiries should be made at the security desk by the main entrance.

John Shaw's Punch House

IN 1738 John Shaw opened a punch house in the 14th-century building which stood on the former market place (today occupied mainly by Marks & Spencer's new store). John Shaw also started the first gentleman's club in Manchester at his punch house where he lived until his death in 1796.

Today John Shaw's Punch House is known as Sinclair's Oyster Bar and it stands on Hanging Ditch, a long-since culverted deep fierce stream (now dried up) which used to tumble over sandstone cliffs into the River Irwell. The original 14th-century four-storey building has been moved and lovingly rebuilt like its black and white timbered neighbour the Old Wellington Inn; but the punch house has also been extended. Together they face the ultra-modern 21st-century glass and chrome edifices of Harvey Nichols and Selfridges stores. The latter is flanked by five slim steel models of wind-power

Sinclair's Oyster Bar in Old Shambles, 1962. (Manchester Archives & Local Studies, Central Library)

Sinclair's Oyster Bar, formerly John Shaw's Punch House, 2003. The inn sign shows his housekeeper, Molly Owen.

windmills (like those which stand on the Yorkshire moors) with small mesh sails, an acknowledgement perhaps of the mediaeval corn mill that once stood near here.

The punch house was first moved in 1971, as part of the Arndale redevelopment scheme in Manchester, and reopened in 1981. On Saturday 15 June 1996 a large bomb exploded on nearby Corporation Street, practically demolishing Marks & Spencer and causing a great deal of damage, although few injuries. Amazingly the old punch house was unaffected by the bomb (which perhaps says something for 14th-century building techniques). However, the punch house was moved again in 1997 to its present position in order to make way for the new Exchange Square development, built in the wake of the bomb's devastation.

Today the bar offers a wide range of alcoholic and non-alcoholic drinks in a variety of sizes, drunk from a glass or a bottle. John Shaw served only punch in china bowls known as 'pees' and 'kews'. 'Pees' were the larger and cost one shilling (one shilling in 1770 = £4.34 at 2002 values); 'kews' were smaller and cost sixpence (sixpence in 1770 = £2.17 at 2002 values). The cost of the drinks must, to some extent, have determined the clientele.

Closing time was 8pm and patrons unwise enough to outstay their welcome were chased away by John Shaw's housekeeper, Molly Owen, brandishing her mop and bucket while giving them the rough edge of her

Plaque on St Ann's church tower giving directions for locating John Shaw's grave.

tongue. No one argued with Molly; they went quietly and quickly if they knew what was good for them. Molly's portrait is depicted on the sign board hanging over the doorway facing Hanging Ditch and Selfridges.

Alcohol other than punch was finally introduced by Joseph Sinclair, who bought the punch house in around 1870 and whose name it still bears. Oysters were first served there in 1848 by the then landlord, a fishmonger called Mr Wadsworth. Oysters are still served today in a variety of dishes ranging from the traditional steak and oyster pie (very warming on a cold winter's day) and Angels and Devils on Horseback (oysters and liver wrapped in bacon, a favourite with Edwardian diners) to oysters mornay and mixed seafood platters with cockles, mussels and oysters. Although still known as an oyster bar, there is a range of other tempting choices on offer, several of which use Mediterranean cooking as an inspiration, and vegetarian dishes are also included.

When John Shaw died he was buried in St Ann's Churchyard. Today the churchyard is paved over and lost, but a plaque on the corner of St Ann's Church tower describes the exact spot when John Shaw lies buried.

A love story and
Little Ireland

IN THE central Manchester suburb of Chorlton-on-Medlock, close to Oxford Road station, a new 'inner city living' project, the Macintosh Village, is being built, centred on the remaining core of Charles Macintosh's mill in the Chorlton Mills complex. Here in 1823 Macintosh developed a process to waterproof cloth using by-products from gas manufacture and used it to make waterproof clothing. Ultimately the firm of Dunlop grew out of this venture. Macintosh Village is an ambitious development of eco-friendly apartments and duplexes, refurbished mills, workshops, studios and café bars, designed, in the words of the construction company, Taylor Woodrow, to 'regenerate, restore and reconnect...' and to provide 'stylish living' using wind power, solar power, sustainable materials and other energy-saving methods.

The complex of mills, in the middle of which the new Macintosh Village is being built, might never have existed but for a tragic love story on a theme

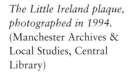

The Little Ireland plaque, photographed in 1994. (Manchester Archives & Local Studies, Central Library)

SITE OF
LITTLE IRELAND
LARGE NUMBERS OF IMMIGRANT
IRISH WORKERS LIVED HERE IN
APPALLING HOUSING CONDITIONS
BUILT   C. 1827
VACATED   C. 1847
DEMOLISHED   C. 1877

which is as old as the hills. In the 18th century the land on which the Chorlton Mills stood was part of the Chorlton Estate owned by the Minshull family. In 1755 Thomas Minshull died and his widow, Lady Minshull, found herself the sole remaining survivor of the family, having lost her only child prematurely. When she was 60 she fell in love with a good-looking 'toy boy', Cornet Roger Aytoun (better known as 'Spanking Roger'), of Inchdarnie, Fifeshire, and in 1769 she married him against the advice of her friends. He then proceeded to spend her fortune and he vandalised the Chorlton Estate by selling it off piecemeal in the 1780s as the cotton mill boom was about to begin. The former Lady Minshull, now Mrs Roger Aytoun, died heartbroken and disillusioned in 1783.

Minshull (sometimes spelled Mynshull) Street, as shown on a map of Manchester in 1794, was renamed Aytoun Street, onto which the Crown Court now faces, and the present Minshull Street, which did not exist in 1794, now runs behind the Crown Court. In 1794 Roger Aytoun also owned much of the land around the former Garrat Hall (which stood on the corner of Granby Row and the present Princess Street).

Some idea of the rapidity of change can be seen in the writings of Thomas de Quincey. He was born in Greenheys (on the edge of Chorlton-on-Medlock near to Hulme, between Oxford Road and Moss Side) in around 1791. De Quincey says that then it was 'separated from Manchester by an entire mile.' At the time of his writing, however, de Quincey says that Greenheys was '...now, and for many a long year, overtaken by the hasty strides of this great city...' and that '...gloomy the streets of Manchester were at that time, mud below, smoke above...' (*Confessions of an English Opium Eater*, 1821)

Chorlton Mills were an important early mill complex and became some of the earliest mills to use steam rather than water power. The earliest mill in Chorlton was built in 1795 on Hulme Street, though the most well known of the Chorlton Mills was Charles Macintosh's Mill. Another mill of note was the Oxford Road Twist Mill, owned and built by Samuel Marsland. Adjacent to this mill stood a mill tenanted by Robert Owen, who would later campaign so vigorously for a reduction in the hours of children working in the mills. Chorlton New Mill, built for Hugh Birley in 1814, is probably the earliest surviving example of a fireproof mill in Manchester.

The success of Chorlton Mills in the 19th century, however, hid a shameful episode in Manchester's social history and one which the new inhabitants of the Macintosh Village may find hard to believe ever took place because their lives will be so different from those who were caught up in this sad story.

The approach to Oxford Road station under the railway bridge from Oxford Road, and the cobbled cul de sac of James Leigh Street at the foot of the bridge, mask the northern border of Little Ireland and recall an almost forgotten nightmare from the days of 'Cottonopolis'. The heart of Little Ireland lay in the millscape of nearby Great Marlborough Street, where a blue plaque on a building now used as an office block commemorates its existence in stark dates:

Little Ireland built *c.*1827
vacated *c.*1847
demolished *c.*1877

The Chorlton Mills complex, which surrounded Little Ireland, was bounded by Cambridge Street, Oxford Road, Chester Street and the River Medlock. To the south-west of Oxford Road, the River Medlock, which passes underneath the road just south of the railway station, curves round as though it were the bottom of a large 'ox-bow'; and the notoriously squalid area of Little Ireland was tucked into the ox-bow where Irish immigrants and refugees scraped a poverty-stricken living as best they could.

However, the low-lying land and the proximity of the mills to the river and dwellings had a disastrous effect on local living conditions:

...a portion of low, swampy ground, liable to be frequently inundated, and to constant exhalation, is included between a high bank over which the Oxford Road passes, and a bend of the river Medlock, where its course is impeded by a weir. This unhealthy spot lies so low that the chimneys of its houses, some of them three stories high, are little above the level of the road. About two hundred of these habitations are crowded together in an extremely narrow space, and they are chiefly inhabited by the lowest Irish. Many of these houses have also cellars, whose floor is scarcely elevated above the level of the water flowing in the Medlock. The soughs are destroyed, or out of repair; and these narrow abodes are in consequence always damp, and are frequently flooded to the depth of several inches, because the surface water can find no exit... it is surrounded on every side by some of the largest factories of the town, whose chimneys vomit forth dense clouds of smoke, which hang heavily over this insalubrious region...
(Sir James Kay-Shuttleworth, Medical Officer of Health *c.*1833)

Absentee landlords and the harsh treatment of the Irish people by William of Orange in the late 1690s had led to increasing poverty and desperation for large numbers of Irish families. Many starved. The coming of the Industrial Revolution and the emergence of 'Cottonopolis' in Manchester seemed to

This plaque on Victorian offices in the heart of the Chorlton Mills complex marks the original site of Little Ireland.

offer the chance of a new life and thousands of Irish people emigrated. Little Ireland was home to the Irish immigrants who came to Manchester looking for work as navvies or in the mills. It was a stain on the social conscience of the city. 1827–1847, the years of occupation for Little Ireland, were before the camera was invented so eye-witness accounts are the main source of evidence for the terrible conditions suffered by the inhabitants.

> *...the most horrible spot... lies on the Manchester side, immediately south-west of Oxford Road, and is known as Little Ireland. In a rather deep hole, in a curve of the Medlock and surrounded on all four sides by tall factories and high embankments, covered with buildings, stand two groups of about two hundred cottages, built chiefly back to back, in which live about four thousand human beings, most of them Irish. The cottages are old, dirty, and of the smallest sort, the streets uneven, fallen into ruts and in part without drains or pavement; masses of refuse, offal and sickening filth lie among standing pools in all directions; the atmosphere is poisoned by the effluvia from these, and laden and darkened by the smoke of a dozen tall factory chimneys. A horde of ragged women and children swarm about here, as filthy as the swine that thrive upon the garbage heaps and in the puddles In short, the whole rookery furnishes such a hateful and repulsive spectacle as can hardly be equalled in the worst court on the Irk...*

> *...for each one hundred and twenty persons, one usually inaccessible privy is provided; and that in spite of all the preachings of the physicians, in spite of the excitement into which the cholera epidemic plunged the sanitary police by reason of the condition of Little Ireland, in spite of everything, in this year of grace 1844, it is in almost the same state as in 1831!*
>
> (Friedrich Engels, *The Condition of the Working Class in England*, Leipzig, 1845)

If the death rate was terrible it seemed that life was worse. The Macintosh Village development, however, will be very different. It will be modern, clean, spacious, environmentally friendly and full of light. Dwellings will have all mod cons, and most will have two toilets each. There will be easy access to local shops and amenities, places of work, entertainment venues, transport and motorways. The quality of life for the Village's future inhabitants will be 'something so completely different' (to misquote Monty Python) that the inhabitants of Little Ireland could not even have dreamed about it; as though the wheel has turned full circle not once but twice.

Mill Living

MANCHESTER and millscapes became synonymous in the 19th century as Manchester made its name and its fortune from the cotton mills; but when the golden age of 'Cottonopolis' ended and the textile industry moved on the mills were left behind. Hundreds of forgotten empty mills with rows of dark windows like unseeing eyes littered the landscape. Thanks to improvements in building regulations and an increasing awareness of health and safety during the latter part of the 19th century the mills were structurally sound and efficiently utilitarian. The simple problem was that no one wanted them.

Some attempts at utilisation were made. A clog mill in Yorkshire; a crafts mill in Delph; a calico mill in Styal; a 'working' mill in Burnley; but these ventures only scratched the surface of the problem of what to do with the empty mills. Then someone discovered that mills have great acoustic qualities and lots of space. Recording studios and music schools and 'cool clubs' moved into Ancoats. The Beehive and Jersey Street mills resounded with noise once more but this time a great deal more melodious than the constant din made by working machinery.

Regeneration is the name of the game for Ancoats, along with several other areas of East Manchester such as Beswick, Bradford, Openshaw, Miles Platting, Clayton and Ardwick. Canals have been cleaned and dredged. Two-up two-down workers' houses, black from decades of grime pumped out by mill chimneys, domestic chimneys and the funnels of steam trains, have been sandblasted and renovated. New businesses are moving in. Extra car parks have been built.

Meanwhile there was still the problem of the remaining 'dark Satanic mills'. There are only so many clogs and crafts, recording studios and cool clubs. It was Ancoats's neighbouring suburb of Miles Platting which first suggested a possible use for the old mills. Miles Platting seems to have taken its name as being the place, about one mile from Manchester, where planks or 'plattings' were laid across Shooter's Brook. Conversion of the mills into

Victoria Mills (then derelict), 1982. (Manchester Archives & Local Studies, Central Library)

flats and apartments seemed an ideal solution to housing being still at a premium in the city with precious little space for new houses and flats, offering both conservation and utilisation of the buildings while at the same time alleviating the problems of accommodation.

Victoria Mills stands on the same road in Miles Platting as the Corpus Christi Basilica and the new library and swimming pool. The mill is characterised by an unusual chimney, shorter than most mill chimneys, which stands on a square brick stack to bring it up to the same height as other mill chimneys, and which is situated in the centre of the building instead of to one side. The ground floor houses an adult education service, a health education centre, offices and a café. Outside, in the former mill yard, there is a large grassed-over area, a children's playground and a car park.

The remaining storeys have been converted into flats and apartments. The central spiral stone staircase curves around a thick brickwork column that has been retained but there are also lifts. Every floor has apartments along each side opening onto a large, square, carpeted lobby broken only by the support pillars of the original mill. The lobby has virtually no natural light because all the windows are enclosed within the apartments. Each floor is colour coded with apartment doors all painted the same colour, but in a different colour for each floor.

The rooms within the apartments are high and narrow, built so that there is one central window within each outer wall. Living rooms and bedrooms face outwards. Fully equipped kitchens, and bathrooms with baths, showers and bidets, are built at the rear, but they are windowless. Many of the fitments are in pine. Some of the apartments have parquet floors and air conditioning. The contrast could not be greater with the hot, humid, dusty, noisy, crowded conditions and the lack of amenities endured by generations of mill workers. There is a certain irony in the fact that the once-hated mills, whose inmates simply wanted to escape from the grim nightmare of intensive textile production where the sun never shone, are now a desirable and sought after commodity offering luxury living accommodation in the heart of a city that is trying to re-invent itself.

Moravian Brothers and Sisters of Fairfield

FAIRFIELD lies on the Manchester–Tameside borders in the heart of the former millscapes about five miles to the east of the city centre. The station area at Fairfield is huge and yet hardly any trains stop there. When it was built there was capacity for several lines and platforms because it was believed in the 1840s that it was where the new Manchester Race Course would be built. That didn't happen and most of Fairfield Station today is scrubby grassland with a couple of forlorn and neglected looking platforms. Fairfield doesn't seem an obvious choice for a place to build a model village on Utopian lines, but that is exactly what happened.

The Moravian Church was founded in 1457 by Jan Hus, a Bohemian martyr and a follower of John Wyclif, and it is said to be the oldest Free Church in northern Europe. Known as the Unitas Fratrum, it flourished in Moravia and Bohemia, now part of modern Czechoslovakia. By the 18th century the Unitas Fratrum were known simply as the Moravians. They were associated with John Wesley for a time and took part in a revival of evangelicalism in England. The Moravian ideals are Christian life and fellowship and they were keen to put their principles into practice.

Initially the Moravian community moved to Dukinfield, but after difficulty with leases they moved to a farm site at Fairfield in 1785 and built their walled model village. It was a self-contained community which produced everything it needed, even the bricks to build the houses and the church. The village included a farm, a bakery, an inn, a shop, a laundry, an inspector of weights and measures, a nightwatchman, a doctor, a fire engine of sorts, an overseer of roads, two boarding schools plus two day schools (one for girls, one for boys) and several workshops. There were also community houses and homes for the 'sisters and brothers' (Single Sisters and Single Brethren as they were known). The settlement was self-contained, self-governed and self-supporting.

Hatting and needlework were two crafts in which the Moravians were skilled. The Sisters produced some lovely and unusual needlework which they sent to Queen Adelaide, wife of King William IV. The Queen liked it so much that she placed regular orders with them. The Brethren baked fresh bread daily and set up a bread delivery service to the surrounding area. These activities gave them trade and contact with their neighbours and they earned respect for their peaceful and law-abiding ways.

The streets were wide and tree-lined, surfaced with cobbles, paving and red gravel. The red-brick Georgian cottages were arranged in a formal pattern along the streets. The main terrace with the church at its centre was flanked by the Girls' School and the Theological College, and faced the church gardens and graveyard. There was a symmetrical unity to the place which was both pleasing and unusual. Even today it retains an 18th century ambience. It was the largest such settlement in Britain and as such is unique in British history.

Time passes and with time comes change. The little community is no longer enclosed or self-contained. There are no farms and meadows any more and

The Moravian settlement in Fairfield, 1970. (Manchester Archives & Local Studies, Central Library)

The Moravian Church for the community at Fairfield, 1986. (Manchester Archives & Local Studies, Central Library)

the nightwatchman has long since gone. The Day Schools closed in 1864. The Boys' Boarding School closed in 1891; the Girls' Boarding School is now Fairfield High School for Girls and open to all. The Moravian Theological College in Fairfield closed in 1958. However, the settlement has survived as an active working and religious community which still practises the same beliefs and principles as those at the settlement's conception in 1785.

The Moravian Reverend Benjamin La Trobe designed and built the Moravian village at Fairfield in 1785. He died just over a year later at the end of 1786. One of his daughters, Mary Agnes La Trobe, married John Bateman. Their son, John La Trobe Bateman, was educated at Fairfield before being apprenticed as a surveyor and engineer. After qualifying he assisted Thomas Ashworth to build the Hurst reservoir at Glossop (about 15 miles from Manchester) in 1831. By 1846 Manchester, like other urban areas, had recognised a desperate need for clean fresh drinking water. John La Trobe Bateman submitted plans for a series of five reservoirs which would run down the Longdendale Valley near Glossop and which would supply all of Manchester's needs for drinking water.

From 1848–77 he designed and built the five reservoirs: Woodhead, Torside and Rhodes Wood for drinking water; Vale House and Bottoms as 'compensation' reservoirs; plus two smaller reservoirs at Hollingworth and Arnfield. He also built a supply system via tunnels from Rhodes Wood to the Godley treatment plant; and three service reservoirs at Godley, Denton and Audenshaw. It is a tribute to his work that the reservoirs and supply systems are still in use in the 21st century. Although beyond the Manchester boundaries, Longdendale, a wild and beautiful valley which stretches to the Yorkshire borders, is a favourite haunt of stressed Mancunians.

Mr Thomas's Chop House

ATALL narrow brick and tiled building with a corner entrance fronts onto Cross Street while the side of the building stretches the length of St Ann's Alley to the 'beer garden' at the rear, situated in the former churchyard of St Ann's. The most remarkable aspect of the building appears to be the somewhat ornate brown tiled frontage and the rounded bay windows, with leaden panes in their upper parts, of the first and second floors. There is a green sign over the door announcing:

Mr Thomas's Chop House

Perhaps this was once part of some eminent Victorian's office or warehouse with the ground floor now converted to a modern pub which serves quick bar food? Nothing could be further from the truth.

The original building was a Georgian town house, the style of which is still evident in the external façade and style of the Chop House. It was first opened as a restaurant and public house in 1867 by Thomas Studd, whose Christian name led to it being called Mr Thomas's Chop House. Chop houses are an old British institution dating back to Stuart times when business dinners consisted simply of large plates of cooked or grilled meat and as much good wine or ale as could decently be drunk.

To step through the door is to step back in time over 100 years; the transition every bit as spectacular as anything offered by Dr Who's Tardis time machine. The interior of the Chop House is decorated with green and white tiles; the arches have darker green tiles of an unusually intense hue; the furniture is dark mahogany; the waiters are traditional in black trousers with white shirts, black waistcoats, white aprons and even a white tea-cloth folded neatly over one arm. The only concession here to the 21st century is that the male and female staff are dressed alike. Women in trousers would have been deemed disgusting beyond belief in Victorian England. There is no canned music, no flashy lighting, no fake beams, and no fast food in sight.

Chop houses, where, by Mr Thomas's time, a gentleman could expect to get a good home-cooked traditional dinner of meat and two or three veg, washed down with a decent claret, and perhaps followed by a good steamed pudding, were very popular in 19th-century England. Charles Dickens would have been at home here; so too would the characters in Conan Doyle's novels of Sherlock Holmes, and the men who traded cotton at Manchester's famous Royal Exchange.

It comes as a slight surprise to learn that much of Mr Thomas's Chop House was not in fact built until 1901, when the building was extended back towards St Ann's churchyard by the architect, Robert Walker, who built a cast-iron frame and then covered it in handcast terracotta and Accrington bricks. The old Queen died in January of that year but early Edwardian England's values were still those of the much-loved Queen. In Manchester, cotton was still king, and the Chop House was still extremely popular.

To keep the flavour of those times the 21st-century chefs have studied the recipe books of their 19th-century counterparts. Traditional Lancashire dishes popular in the time of 'Cottonopolis' include thick brown soups; oysters; black pudding; hotpot; steak and kidney pudding; potato cakes; bacon and cabbage; fish pies; steamed fruit puddings with custard; mature cheeses and good strong chutneys; and they are all highly favoured dishes on today's old time menu. Lip service has been paid to 21st century tastes in the form of fresh herb dressings, spicy custards, and the addition of vegetarian dishes such as wild mushroom risotto (risotto being a good old Victorian stand-by for using leftover meats) and baked Irish cheeses with date chutney.

In summer diners can have their meals served outside in the 'beer garden' at the rear of the Chop House. The tables and chairs are laid out on paving stones which hide the graves of the former incumbents of St Ann's churchyard. Enjoying roast lamb and plum pudding barely seven or eight feet above yesterday's skeletons might be thought to show a lack of taste, but curiously there seems nothing incongruous about it. Especially when the sun is shining and a street musician can be heard in St Ann's Square. Life, as they say, must go on.

Mr Thomas's Chop House on Cross Street, photographed in 1970. (Manchester Archives & Local Studies, Central Library)

Northern Quarter

T HE TERM 'Northern Quarter' is a modern misnomer since it does not denote the northern part of the city or even the actual northern part of the city centre. Far from being anywhere near a quarter, it is simply an area within the northern part of the central city which is trying to reinvent itself as 'a funky place where it's cool'. It does not include neighbouring Ancoats,

The old exterior of the Printworks building, 1991. (Manchester Archives & Local Studies, Central Library)

which lies adjacent and forms a larger part of the northern inner city. Roughly speaking the Northern Quarter is bounded by Oldham Street, Swan Street, Shude Hill, Withy Grove and High Street.

Oldham Street has an unmistakable air of having seen better days and its chief feature is probably the Methodist Central Hall; for years a focus for political, social, educational and community activities as well as a gathering place for religious worship. Otherwise the street seems to offer a mish-mash of wig shops, textile shops, costume hire shops and music shops. However, fancy dress shops are hard to find and maybe they and the music and the wig hire places contribute to the generally bohemian air of the Northern Quarter.

From Market Street to the Church Street junction on Tib Street is fairly unremarkable except for a nail salon and Starbucks Coffee Shop. Tib Street, with its underground river, was formerly renowned for pet shops but now the street could perhaps be said to be the most bohemian of all the Northern Quarter. However Holland Hydroponics (and exotic pets) keeps part of the tradition alive with a lush underwater mural painted across three double windows. Tib Street is one of those taking part in the Northern Quarter Artworks Scheme which also includes Thomas Street and Oldham Street.

On the corner of Tib Street and Church Street is a Victorian red-brick

The wholesale fish market
in the Northern Quarter,
1966. (Manchester
Archives & Local Studies,
Central Library)

edifice that might be termed a folly, but which is actually the ruined corner of a former warehouse. Crowning it is a metal sculpture which could be a modern art representation of Dixieland jazz with its umbrellas and stray musical note emerging from a large funnel, which might be the disproportionate end of a snaking clarinet slithering along the edge of the brickwork; the whole perhaps executed in that fashion as a tribute to the Industrial Revolution. The artist is David Kemp and it is known as the Tib Street Horn and it dominates the local scene, complements Affleck's Palace opposite and dwarfs the tiny fresh food market on the opposite pavement.

Further down, painted ceramic tiles by Estelle Hayes make up a mural on the wall of the car park commemorating a circus which used to perform there. Nearby is Affleck's Palace on the corner of Short Street. It is a rambling red-brick converted Victorian warehouse which offers '...alternative shopping and high fashion on four floors including clothes, shoes, jewellery, records and a café...' The ground floor windows are boarded and covered in 'magic' artwork. Huge street lamps, fashioned in cast iron like gracefully drooping daffodils, hang from second floor level. There is a notice outside the main entrance which reads: 'And on the sixth day God created MANchester'.

Thomas Street is next left off Tib Street after Church Street. It is worth walking the full length of Tib Street to Swan Street to appreciate the mix of old and new and the impromptu artistic work, like wall murals of modern millscapes or those featuring Tib Street's history, that makes Tib Street so colourful. Return to the Thomas Street junction doing the archaeologist's walk (head down looking at the ground) and read the quotes and inscriptions worked into the pavement slabs. Some are brief, some are deep, and some are philosophical.

The Manchester Craft Centre lies in Thomas Street, just off Oak Street. Before the Industrial Revolution oak trees stood here in the meadows alongside the River Tib. There are two floors of craft studios and workshops plus a wholefood café. The artistes and craftsmen work on the premises and there is a nice community feel to the place. The main problem is that it is off the general 'beaten track' and visitors need to know their way around central Manchester and preferably be on foot. The same can be said for the new Chinese Arts Centre further down Thomas Street, almost to the junction with High Street. The centre is a veritable treasure trove of things Chinese: books, music, art, photography, and a genuine traditional Chinese tea room. Many of the books and notices are in Chinese but there are notices in English too when it matters. The Chinese gallery at the rear has thoughtful photographic studies of landscapes and Chinese people. It is a peaceful and welcoming place in which to relax.

Affleck's Palace in Tib Street, photographed in 1995. (Manchester Archives & Local Studies, Central Library)

Backing onto the Chinese Arts Centre in typically English fashion are the former wholesale fish markets. The fish markets front onto High Street and an inscription on the somewhat ornate façade proclaims that they were first opened on 14 February 1873. Inside a very modern 'residential commercial retail centre' has been developed which backs, appropriately enough, onto Salmon Street. The cobbled street in front of the fish markets may be original but it is not entirely at ease with the surrounding 'designer' apartments.

From the fish markets it is only a short distance to Shude Hill and to Withy (willow) Grove, believed to be the source of the lost River Dene which is said to have run through Hanging Ditch. A pub called the Rovers Return, a name well known to all *Coronation Street* fans, was built in 1306 and used to stand on Shude Hill. There is also a commemorative plaque remembering food riots, by citizens asking for fair prices for food, which took place on Shude Hill in 1757. It reads:

One of several food riots took place here.
Four people died and fifteen were injured during the night of
14th–15th November 1757

The plaque commemorating food riots in Shude Hill. (Manchester Archives & Local Studies, Central Library)

In 1780 Richard Arkwright built a mill near Shude Hill on adjoining Miller Street. It was the only cotton mill in Manchester. It was a five-storey building 200ft (60m) long and 30ft (9m) wide. The mill has not survived but the area around Kelvin Street has a number of domestic, industrial and commercial buildings from this period.

Withy Grove (with not even a hint of the willow trees now) runs down to Corporation Street. Between Dantzic Street and Corporation Street on Withy Grove stands the Printworks, formerly the Withy Grove Press, which was the largest press plant in Europe. It was acquired by Robert Maxwell in the early 1980s and was renamed Maxwell House. The *Daily Mirror* newspaper was printed here until 1986. By 1987 the printworks was closed and derelict. It suffered severe damage from the terrorist bomb explosion in 1996. This resulted in an urban regeneration programme under which the Printworks was completely transformed.

Today the Printworks is like a small enclosed village of café society. There are 'pavement' bars and cafés like Norwegian Blue and the Hard Rock Café; pubs and clubs such as Babushka and Tiger, Tiger; a 20-screen cinema complex (the Filmworks) and a casino (the Hard Rock Casino). There is also a bookshop, designer shops and a health club. The Printworks lies right at the heart of what has been described as Manchester's 'vibrant and volatile' club scene.

If it had still existed, Poet's Corner would have been an ideal addition to the Northern Quarter, although it lay technically outside the 'boundary'.

The Rovers Return in Shude Hill, built 1306. (Manchester Archives & Local Studies, Central Library)

Poet's Corner became the nickname of the Rising Sun public house on Long Millgate which stood almost opposite the entrance to Chetham's. Long Millgate has been severely curtailed in recent times so that only a fraction of the original street remains. The Rising Sun was, at one time, reputed to be the oldest building in Manchester; a black and white timbered building in the mediaeval style with the first floor built out over the ground floor. It

Tib Street Horn by David Kemp, corner of Tib Street and Church Street, 2003.

was demolished in 1923 because it had become structurally unsafe. One of the late 18th/early 19th-century landlords was a poet and he encouraged other poets to meet at the pub. They discussed poetry over their ale until the early hours; sometimes reading to each from their work. From somewhere they found the money to publish one or two pamphlets of their poetry. Then the poetic landlord died. His successor decided that poetry wasn't for real men and banned the remaining poets from holding meetings in his pub. Unfortunately there appears to be no trace of the pamphlets they published and so it seems that their work is lost.

The present Northern Quarter is somewhat different from that which Engels knew 150 years ago:

> *...the Old Town, which lies between the northern limit of the commercial quarter and the River Irk. Here even the better streets, such Todd Street, Long Millgate, Withy Grove, and Shudehill are narrow and tortuous. The houses are dirty, old, and tumble-down.*

Holland Hydroponics, Tib Street. Tib Street used to be full of pet shops.

Wall mural on Tib Street reflecting the history of the street.

The side streets have been built in a disgraceful fashion. If one enters the district near the 'Old Church' and goes down Long Millgate, one sees immediately on the right hand side a row of antiquated houses where not a single front wall is standing upright. This is a remnant of the old Manchester of the days before the town became industrialised. The original inhabitants and their children have left for better houses in other districts, while the houses in Long Millgate, which no longer satisfied them, were left to a tribe of workers containing a strong Irish element. Here one is really and truly in a

Affleck's Palace on Tib Street, 2003.

district which is quite obviously given over entirely to the working classes, because even the shopkeepers and the publicans of Long Millgate make no effort to give their establishments a semblance of cleanliness. The condition of this street may be deplorable, but it is by no means as bad as the alleys and courts which lie behind it, and which can be approached only by covered passages so narrow that two people cannot pass. Anyone who has never visited these courts and alleys can have no idea of the fantastic way in which the houses have been packed together in disorderly confusion in impudent defiance of all reasonable principles of town planning. And the fault lies not merely in the survival of old property from earlier periods in Manchester's history...

(Friedrich Engels, *Condition of the Working Classes in England,* 1844)

Old
Wellington Inn

T HE OLD WELLINGTON Inn stands at right angles to Sinclair's Oyster Bar, formerly John Shaw's Punch House. The inn is a three-storey timbered and gabled building with mullion-style windows. Inside it is satisfyingly warm and cosy and welcoming; full of dark beams and low doorways. Anyone over 5ft 10in (1.75m) in height would be advised to

'duck or grouse'. There are steep crooked stairs leading to an upper floor full of little rooms, some with easy chairs, ideal for quiet or intimate conversations, much as it might have been in the days of John Shaw's gentleman's club.

The exact age of the building is uncertain but it is known to have existed in 1552 during the reign of Edward VI. In 1554 it was purchased, together with what is now Sinclair's, by the Byrom family, and the ground floor was used as a linen drapers shop. John Byrom was born in what is now the Old Wellington Inn, but which was then a private house, on Leap Year's Day (29 February) 1692. Educated at Cambridge, he gained the degree of MA and then he married his cousin, Miss Elizabeth Byrom, against much family opposition. He invented a system of phonetic shorthand which was a forerunner of the better known Pitman's shorthand, and made his living by teaching shorthand. In 1723 he was elected a Fellow of the Royal Society and in 1724 he inherited the family estate on the death of his brother. As a middle-aged man in 1745 he watched Bonnie Prince Charlie's triumphant march into Manchester from his home in the present Old Wellington Inn. He also was an accomplished poet and linguist whose writings included *Colin and Phoebe* and the hymn *Christians Awake*. John Byrom died on 26 September 1763.

The Old Wellington Inn off Exchange Square near the Cathedral, 2003. John Byrom lived in the house during the 18th century.

In 1830 the owner of the house obtained a licence to sell alcohol. At first the new inn was called the Vintners Arms and then subsequently Kenyon's Vaults. By 1865 the ground floor was established as the Wellington Inn while the upper floors housed mathematical and optical instrument makers. In 1897 the upper floors were taken over by the Olde Fyshing Tackle Shop. The building was raised 4ft 9in (1.4m) in 1974 as part of the Arndale development in Manchester city centre. The IRA bomb of 1996 caused some damage and in February 1997 it was decided to move the building 300m to its present position to accommodate the new Exchange Square development. Work was completed in 1999 and the Old Wellington Inn reopened in November of that year.

Today the Old Wellington Inn is a very popular pub restaurant in the city centre, which specialises in al fresco eating when the weather permits. Most of those enjoying their meals and drinks at the rustic wooden tables on the large paved patio in front of the inn are probably unaware that in mediaeval times a corn mill stood close by. The mill belonged to the Lords of Manchester and by the 12th century all their tenants, even from as far away as Blackley, Gorton or Withington, were required to bring their corn to this mill for grinding and to hand over a portion of the ground corn as payment for the service.

Ordsall Hall

TO INCLUDE Ordsall Hall in *Hidden Manchester* is perhaps cheating slightly, since Ordsall Hall lies just across the River Irwell in Salford. However, Manchester and Salford have long been twin cities, merging into each other close to Manchester city centre; and in earlier times Manchester was actually included in the Salford Hundred. The hidden story is that Ordsall Hall plays a key part in Manchester becoming the textile centre of the world in Victorian times because the Radclyffe family of Ordsall Hall (together with a little help from Edward III) were responsible for the development of a skilled and structured textile industry in the north-west in the 13th century, which laid the foundations for the amazing success of 19th-century 'Cottonopolis'.

Ordsall Hall lies not far from what is now Salford Quays, close to a bend in the River Irwell. *Ord* is Old English for a sword or a point (sometimes of land like a ridge) and *halh* means an enclosure. The first mention of Ordsall comes in 1177 when feudal dues were paid by Ordeshala. In 1354 when Sir John de Radclyffe finally established his title to the manor of Ordsall it consisted of the hall and its grounds, 120 acres of farming land, 12 acres of woodlands and 12 acres of meadow. He enlarged and improved the hall, transforming the place into a 'desirable residence' of its day so that it had five bedrooms, a large dining hall, kitchen, new chapel (licensed in 1361), a dovecote, an orchard, a windmill, three granges ('home farms' producing food solely for the use of the hall); two shippons (cattle sheds), and a garner (granary).

Sir John fought alongside Edward III in France and distinguished himself in battle at Caen, Crècy and Calais. In recognition of his services the King rewarded him and asked if there were any additional favours he would like granted. Like Edward, Sir John had been extremely impressed by the skills of the Flemish weavers he had encountered while fighting on the Continent and he requested permission for some of them to accompany him on his return to England. There were linen and woollen industries in the north-west of England, as there were in East Anglia, but English weaving skills were poor and textiles from the Manchester area were considered to be of particularly inferior quality.

The Flemish weavers Sir John brought back with him were settled on the Ordsall Hall estate. He built comfortable small cottages for the weavers and instructed them that, in return, as well as weaving their cloth, they were to teach their English counterparts their weaving skills. The Flemish were also skilled in silk weaving and so began a small silk industry in the Manchester area. Four hundred years later the silk industry would prove to be the foundation for the cotton industry; but even by Tudor times the Manchester textile industry was well established thanks to the Flemish weavers and their descendants. Manchester 'cottons' (actually a napped woollen weave) and Manchester 'small wares' (ribbons, garters, laces, etc) were popular and in Elizabeth I's reign an Act was passed regulating their production. Coincidentally, during this period Margaret de Radclyffe (d.1599) was the Queen's favourite Maid of Honour.

Early the following century the hall was caught up in a love story that might be just that; a fictional romance which only ever existed in the mind of a Victorian novelist, but there are enough elements of truth in it to suggest that it may not just be fiction, but based on folklore of an actual half-remembered event.

Novelist Harrison Ainsworth was born and brought up in early 19th-century Manchester, attending Manchester Grammar School and spending much of his boyhood rambling around the local countryside and seeing the old Halls such as Ordsall, Hulme and Garrat. He grew up to become a prolific writer and in 1841 he published a novel called *Guy Fawkes*.

The novel is based on a local legend that Ordsall Hall was where Guy Fawkes and Robert Catesby hatched the Gunpowder Plot, intended to blow up the Houses of Parliament and the unpopular King James I. While at Ordsall, Fawkes is said to have fallen in love with Viviana, the daughter of the house, who was later tortured and then died after refusing to reveal details of the Gunpowder Plot. Robert Catesby was also in love with Viviana and so too was Humphrey Chetham (who founded Chetham's Library). The book also includes the legend that Guy Fawkes fled the King's troopers by using underground passages which led from the Hall to an inn on Withy Grove in what is now Manchester city centre.

The north-west was a strongly Catholic area and the Radclyffes were staunch Catholics (and heavily fined for it), although they professed loyalty to the sovereign of the day. Catesby was a member of a prominent Northamptonshire family who were also Catholics. He had been involved in the rebellion led by the Earl of Essex against Queen Elizabeth I, and he had also been accused of trying to poison the Queen. It is quite possible that the two families knew each other and perhaps Robert was offered a temporary sanctuary at Ordsall Hall when life became uncomfortable for him in London. If he, and his friend, Fawkes, were going to hatch such a daring plot, Ordsall Hall was a good place to do it, among friends and at a safe distance from London.

There is no record of a Viviana Radclyffe but there are such things as poetic license and changing names. There was a Jane Radclyffe who was about 30 years old in 1605. She was the sister of Sir John Radclyffe who then owned Ordsall Hall. She was also married, to Sir Ralph Constable, but that is not to say that she could not, or would not, have fallen in love with Guy Fawkes. It would also be an excellent reason for Ainsworth not using her real name. Humphrey Chetham was a friend of the family but there is no record of him falling in love with one of its female members. He was also still quite young at the time, having not been born until 1580.

Underground passages from the Hall to Manchester did exist. In April 1900 the *Manchester Guardian* published a letter which said:

> *...I was shown a door in Hanging Bridge Hotel cellar where the arches could be seen and a door made up...it was the entrance to an underground passage under the Irwell...to...Ordsall Hall...the owner had not traversed the passage himself, but the previous owner had, but had to turn back because of bad smells...*

Manchester Notes and Queries for November 1901 published the following fragment:

> *...when the licensed house at the Cathedral end of Hanging Bridge* [which would have been almost on Withy Grove] *was rebuilt, a tunnel was found with five or six skeletons with fragments of clothing and copper coin with Latin inscription...*

This was said to be copper coinage, probably from the reign of Queen Mary Tudor and her husband, King Philip II of Spain (1553–8); barely half a century before the Gunpowder Plot.

There is enough to suggest that, maybe, just maybe, Fawkes and Catesby sat together, perhaps in the Star Chamber at the Hall, whispering about an impossible dream of blowing up the King and Parliament which would free the Catholics from persecution. Their host, Sir John Radclyffe, might well have known nothing about it. Both of them may have been in love with the same woman, either a Radclyffe lady or someone else close to the family, whose identity was enigmatically disguised like Shakespeare's 'dark lady' of

Ordsall Hall and the cruck gate, 1900. (Manchester Archives & Local Studies, Central Library)

the sonnets. It is also more than possible that one, or both of them, did hide somewhere in the hall from the King's troopers and then made their way into Manchester via a labyrinthine network of underground tunnels and passages. To whom did the skeletons, discovered in the tunnel near Withy Grove in the late 19th century, belong?

Ordsall Hall of course has a ghost. It is inconceivable that a house with such a history would not have attracted some haunting tales. The White Lady is usually said to appear in the Great Hall or the Star Chamber. Her identity is unknown, though she is popularly believed to be Margaret Radclyffe, Queen Elizabeth's Maid of Honour, who died of 'a broken heart' in 1599 after her twin brother, Alexander, was killed at sea. Some, however, believe that she is the ghost of the mystery lady with whom Guy Fawkes fell in love.

The later 19th century saw the once moated Hall in its well-kept rural environs surrounded by the millscapes with their belching manufactories and rows of grimy worker's cottages. In 1875 the once proud and beautiful building became a Working Men's Club for employees of Haworth's Mill, bringing a brutal end to the centuries of intrigue and romance. It could be considered fitting though that the former home of the man who established the textile industry in the north-west during the 13th century should become an integral part of the 19th-century textile industry. The Hall, however, survived and today it is known as the Ordsall Hall Museum. Much restoration work was undertaken before it was opened to the public and it is well worth a visit.

Peterloo

IT HAS become Manchester's hidden tragedy; such a shameful atrocity in British social history that even today, nearly 200 years later, there are still those who seek to deny it ever happened. There is no official memorial, save an insignificant plaque, to mark the spot, yet so strong was the folk memory that until the 1980s there was a great reluctance to use mounted police in Manchester. The Peterloo Massacre took place on 16 August 1819 and was given the name by a witness who had fought at Waterloo a few years earlier because St Peter's Fields strongly resembled a battlefield with dead and injured people lying everywhere after the massacre had taken place.

In 1819 St Peter's Fields (taking their name from the church which stood on the site of the Cenotaph in St Peter's Square) covered the area which today includes Peter Street, the Midland Hotel, the GMEX, the Free Trade Hall and Central Library. Sunday 16 August was the date set for several speakers, who included Henry Hunt, Richard Carlile and Samuel Bamford, to hold a public meeting at which they would address the crowd on issues of unfair working practices, the need for reform and radical ideas for the way forward; or in the jargon of the day, '…calling for reforms to conditions which condemned thousands to a life of poverty, wretchedness, tyranny and injustice'. It was estimated that this meeting might attract a crowd of some 60,000–80,000 people, who would come from Manchester and the surrounding towns and villages to hear the speakers.

In 1819 16 August was a warm sunny day. Interest and curiosity was uppermost in the minds of people attending; not militancy; plus the unaccustomed excitement of a day out. Men brought their wives and families. Women dressed themselves and their children in Sunday best clothes for this unexpected treat. Men wore their best fustian suits. They 'marched' into Manchester in the manner of those following a carnival procession; laughing, joking, gossiping with people they knew, some singing, some waving flags.

The local authorities, however, were becoming nervous. It was only 30 years since the French Revolution and those in power were still badly unsettled by workers' meetings and talk of reform and any possible alteration (or threat as they saw it) to the social order. The magistrates therefore arranged for about 1,200 cavalry (from the 15th Hussars, the Manchester and Salford Yeomanry, the Cheshire Yeomanry and the Royal Horse Artillery), several hundred infantrymen and 400 special constables to be on duty that day. At about 11am on the Sunday morning 10 local magistrates met at Mr Buxton's home. He had a house on Mount Street which overlooked St Peter's Fields. It would have stood approximately on the site occupied today by Television House and Starbucks coffee shop.

The crowd was entirely peaceful but growing rapidly. William Hulton, the chairman of the magistrates, then ordered the Boroughreeve (the early 19th-century equivalent of a modern chief superintendent of police) and the 400 special constables to clear a path between the magistrates' house and the hustings from which the guest speakers would address the meeting. When the speakers arrived at about 1.20pm the crowd was some 80,000 strong, but peaceful and good-natured. At this point nerves took over from common sense. The magistrates decided that '...the town was in great danger...' and ordered the arrest of the speakers. The deputy constable said that this could not be done without military assistance. Hulton wrote the necessary letters of authority and the cavalry were sent in.

What happened next was horrific. The cavalry knew that they were heavily outnumbered so they decided on charge and slash tactics rather than trying to disperse the crowd peacefully. People attending the meeting were neither armed nor prepared for militancy and violence. The cavalry charged into the crowd, slashing wildly to the right and left with their sabres. Those who have been in a large crowd will know how difficult, if not impossible, it is to move quickly, if at all. Total panic ensued. Women were slashed across their breasts and stomachs, blood pouring down their pretty Sunday dresses. Children were crushed and killed by the horses' hooves. Men were sabred and then trampled. People fled wildly in all directions, screaming with terror. Within 10 minutes St Peter's Fields were empty except for the dead and injured. By their actions the cavalry had killed about 20 men, women and children, and injured over 400 people.

The speakers were arrested and imprisoned. The magistrates were congratulated on their excellence for taking the action that they had. The Government attempted to suppress news of the massacre and when that failed carried out a 'white-washing exercise'. Authors of pamphlets giving a true account of Peterloo were arrested and imprisoned. There was, and still is, controversy over what happened. However there is one piece of evidence that cannot be denied. John Rylands Library on Deansgate holds the original death and injuries compensation book for Peterloo. Compiled in 1820, it details the names, addresses and ages of those who died or were injured, the injuries they received, and the amount of compensation paid to them and their families. The fact that compensation was paid at all is a corporate admission of guilt, or at least of some responsibility.

The ordinary working folk of Manchester never forgot or forgave Peterloo: an unprovoked massacre of unarmed civilians by their fellow countrymen. The civic authorities were made to realise that such a thing must never happen again. For 150 years after the massacre the sight of mounted uniforms in Manchester was sufficient to cause intense public unease. In other cities mounted police were used for crowd control and public events, but not in Manchester until the closing decades of the 20th century. The folk memory of Peterloo was too strong. In time building development covered the fields where the tragedy had happened. Central Library disguised the spot from which some of the cavalry had charged. Peter Street, the Midland Hotel and the Free Trade Hall hid the scene of the carnage. Although there is no proper memorial to those who suffered at Peterloo, a digitised copy of the deaths and injuries compensation book can be found online at www.spinningtheweb.org.uk and that is its own sad memorial to a tragedy which should never have happened.

Extracts from the Peterloo Compensation Book 1820

Mary Fildes   Cornet Street Beswick
...was much beat by constables and leaped off the hustings... 40/- [£91.60]

Margaret Booth   126 Ancoats Lane
...much trampled on, 9 weeks confined, back and sides still sore... 20/- [£45.80] + 10/- [£22.90]

Samuel Ackerley   3 Grigson Street Deansgate
...a sabre cut on his left leg, knocked down and trampled on... 11 years of age...20/- [£45.80]

James Bell   Ancoats Lane near the Hall
...a weaver, crushed and thrown down, disabled a month, his loins still painful... 20/- [£45.80]

William Barnes   7 Ancoats Street
...crushed in breast by the crowd and trampled, a very poor and wretched old man of 60... 20/- [£45.80]

Nancy Jackson   no address given
...her elbow broke, was taken to the infirmary, a weaver with four children, very poor... 20/- [£45.80]

Edward Johnson   67 Henry Street
...trod on by the cavalry and 2 ribs fractured, a weaver 50 years of age... 20/- [£45.80]

Rich Wilde   9 Coop Street, Swan Street
...a boy cut on the back of the head severely... 20/- [£45.80]

John Rhodes   3 Pitts Hopwood
...sabre cut on the head by which he lost much blood... a woman... shaved the hair and put on a plaister... he was dreadfully bruised internally so that he has not since held up his head... and died about the 18th November [1819]...To his father 66/- [£151.14]

Platt Hall

PLATT HALL lies in Platt Fields just at the end of the 'curry mile' (so called because of the large number of excellent Indian restaurants) in Rusholme; on the No.42 bus route towards Didsbury. Platt is a mediaeval name for a small piece of ground and Platt Fields were held by the Knights Hospitallers of St John of Jerusalem in the 12th century. The first Platt Hall was a late mediaeval lath and plaster building although its exact date isn't known. When it came into the possession of the de la Mores they changed their family name to Platt. In 1625, The Platt, as the house was by then known, was sold to Ralph Worsley, a local merchant.

His son, Charles, was a Major-General in Cromwell's army and became the first MP for Manchester, elected in 1654. Manchester was the only town in Lancashire to support the Puritans, and there was a statue of Oliver Cromwell outside Manchester Cathedral until the 20th century when it was removed to Wythenshawe Hall, where it still stands today. When Cromwell took the mace, the 'bauble' as he termed it, from the House of Commons, he gave it to his close friend, Charles Worsley, and ordered him to keep it at The

Rusholme, 1900. A bakery van in a country lane. (Manchester Archives & Local Studies, Central Library)

Haymaking at Platt Hall, 1900. (Manchester Archives & Local Studies, Central Library)

Platt. It remained there for three months before Worsley was asked to return it to Parliament.

The present Platt Hall is a three-storey red-brick Georgian house built in the early 1760s in the 'Palladian' style; that is symmetrical in appearance with the main building equally flanked by smaller buildings. The smaller buildings at Platt Hall contained the kitchens and the stables. To step into Platt Hall is

The statue of Abraham Lincoln at Platt Hall, 1955. (Manchester Archives & Local Studies, Central Library)

Costumes from the 18th century on display at the hall, 1970. (Manchester Archives & Local Studies, Central Library)

The Platt Unitarian Chapel in Rusholme, 1975. (Manchester Archives & Local Studies, Central Library)

to step into another age. The house is quiet and pleasing, comfortable and gracious; the main staircase sweeping upwards from the wide entrance hall. Original decorative plaster work has been retained and Worsley family portraits hang on the walls of the top floor. During the series of earthquakes which struck Manchester in 2003, Platt Hall found itself close to the epicentre of one of the stronger and longer quakes. It is a testament to the design of the hall that the building inclined slightly but there was no structural damage; just a little plaster dust and a few frayed nerves.

Today the hall, which stands at right-angles to Wilmslow Road and still enjoys an open outlook across Platt Fields, houses the Platt Hall Museum of English Costume. The collection of men's, women's and children's costumes (dating from 1600–1990) is one of the largest in the country. Costume galleries displaying themed exhibitions occupy the ground and first floors while the second floor houses the library and the costume archives. Costume treasures include a dainty pinkish brown 'pet-en-lair' jacket which belonged to the wife of the famous 18th-century actor David Garrick, and a banyan (morning or dressing gown) said to have been given by George III to his Lord Chamberlain. Among the curiosities are crinolines, combinations, corsets and a pretty pair of blue and white stockings knitted by a German girl from Westphalia for her wedding in the 1840s.

Although the American Civil War caused a five-year cotton famine, with mills going on short time working or closing altogether, and brought the beginning of the end for the British cotton industry, the cotton workers of Manchester staunchly supported the cause for the abolition of slavery, despite their own working conditions being little better and sometimes worse than those of the slaves. Abraham Lincoln was so moved by their sufferings during the cotton famine that he sent the cotton workers a personal message of thanks. This is engraved on the plinth of a statue of Abraham Lincoln which stood in front of the Platt Hall until 1986 when it was moved to Lincoln Square close to Manchester Town Hall.

Quarry Bank Mill – the hidden millscape

THE CANDLES flickered as the machinery whirred and clanked, the noise almost overwhelming. Small shadowy figures darted about. The floor was wooden, and slippery with oil and grease. Outside the wind rattled the windows which lined either side of the long room. The spinning mules stretched away into the darkness. Suddenly there was a child's scream. Somewhere in the gloom another child screamed in sympathy. Someone dashed through the mill at speed and everyone turned, startled.

As the lights went up some of the older members among those gathered looked a little sheepish. The 21st-century actresses recreating a story from the 18th century in the spinning room at Quarry Bank Mill for Hallowe'en had perhaps been a little too successful; but for those few minutes their audience had been with them, back in the days of 1795, when children as young as seven or eight worked 12 hours a day in the mill and lived in the nearby purpose-built Apprentice House, far from their family and friends. In most mills children made up the majority of the workforce because they were more nimble than adults and could tie up broken threads quickly; they were smaller and could crawl under the moving machinery to clean up cotton waste; and simply because they were cheap labour.

It is somewhat ironic for Manchester that its only remaining working mill should actually lie two miles outside the city boundary. Quarry Bank Mill once lay in remote countryside totally isolated from the city of the millscapes where '...you hear nothing but the breathing of the vast machines sending forth fire and smoke through their tall chimneys...' (Leon Faucher, *Manchester in 1844*) and the main cotton mill districts, where all the spinning and weaving of cotton was carried out, clustered around the centre of

Manchester on the inner east and south sides of the city containing '...the great mass of smoky, dingy, sweltering and toiling Manchester...' (Angus Bethune Reach, 1849–50), in which the smoke from the mill chimneys was so thick that it often almost blotted out the sun:

> *...the volumes of smoke, which, in spite of legislation to the contrary, continually issue from factory chimneys, and form a complete cloud over Manchester... the enjoyment of the inhabitants would be greatly increased could they breathe a purer atmosphere and have a brighter and more frequent sight of the sun...*
> (Archibald Prentice, 1826).

Quarry Bank Mill still lies in countryside, protected by the National Trust, on the outskirts of Styal village, a short bus ride from Manchester Airport. The mill stands on the banks of the River Bollin at the end of a narrow country lane and is completely hidden from the main road. It was built in 1784 by Samuel Greg. The Gregs considered themselves Manchester mill men and owned several other mills in the Manchester area.

Although the mill was built on the same lines as other early Manchester mills it didn't seem quite so forbidding because of its location and because it was a single entity. The chimney did 'issue forth volumes of smoke' but this was dispersed because of the mill's isolation. The Bollin was not polluted by scores of other mills or dye works along its banks and sometimes, on summer evenings after they had finished work, some of the children were allowed to bathe in the river.

The Gregs were reasonably fair employers; especially for their times. Samuel Greg realised that underfed, over-worked and over-tired children were not going to be as willing or efficient as those who were given adequate food and allowed reasonable rest periods. The children of today would no doubt consider that working 60 hours a week with only one decent meal plus two helpings of porridge (sometimes onion flavoured) a day is not just unreasonable but could actually be considered child abuse. However, in the cotton mill world of the 1790s these children were the lucky ones.

The Apprentice House at Quarry Bank Mill survives and has been restored to how it would have looked during the early 19th century. There are regular guided tours by staff in period costume who explain what the children's lives here were like as they show visitors the kitchen, schoolroom, dormitories, doctor's surgery and the 'house parent's parlour'. It is a 'hands-on' experience. Children and adults alike are invited to take part in lessons using real quill pens (it is incredibly difficult to write properly with them); feel the texture of the porridge which was always made solid enough to be eaten with their hands as the children worked; and to examine the doctor's remedies, including the live leeches (used for 'bleeding' sick children), which frequently escape from their bowl of water.

The apprentices worked from 6am–6pm Monday to Saturday. There were no night shifts. After supper each evening they received two hours basic schooling so that they would learn how to read and write and understand how to do simple maths. On Sunday mornings they attended church and were then given a dinner which usually included some meat. In the afternoon the girls learned embroidery while the boys worked in the kitchen gardens. Sleeping accommodation was in little truckle beds (two to a bed) in segregated dormitories. The surgery was upstairs and the doctor called in regularly.

In the kitchen gardens food was grown to feed the apprentices and herbs were grown for both culinary and medical uses. The gardens are maintained today as they were when the apprentice boys tended the fruit and vegetables, herbs and flowers themselves. Visitors can walk around the gardens and the orchard on narrow grassy paths. The outdoor toilets also survive; one for the boys and one for the girls, built back to back in the garden behind the Apprentice House; a fierce reminder of the discomforts suffered in the days before 'en-suite'. The Apprentice House could hold up to 100 children so many would have to wait their turn; which can't have been much fun, especially at 5 o'clock on a winter's morning.

There are also guided tours through the mill where the children worked; taking visitors through the entire cycle of cotton manufacture from the bales of cotton arriving at the mill, through the cleaning, carding, spinning, weaving, bleaching and dyeing processes to the production of the cotton calico that is sold in the mill shop.

The cotton production machinery used mostly dates from the late 19th and early 20th century and the noise is such that the mill is reluctant to expose visitors to the spinning or weaving sheds for more than 10 minutes. That is long enough to give an understanding of what working in the cotton mills meant for thousands of people.

A large working water-wheel at the mill sometimes powers the looms. There is a weir on the River Bollin just upstream from the mill and then the river flows past the mill and under a wooden footbridge. Across this bridge is the mill meadow, which is a beautiful place to wander in spring and summer. It leads up to the weir and gives a good view of the whole mill complex settled snugly in the valley. There are also walks in the woods and across the fields which surround the mill. Compared to Ancoats (the world's first industrial suburb, now the world's first urban village), Quarry Bank Mill shows just how different cotton production and cotton workers' lives could be within the same city.

The world of the
lost River Tib

L OST RIVERS, canals, streams and brooks seem to make up much of
Manchester's underworld, quite literally. Rivers may flow underground
naturally and in many towns and cities have been partly culverted to ease
building development plans and traffic flow, but they emerge into daylight
again at some point suitable to both the rivers and the people who live on or
over them. In Manchester, however, land was at such a premium during the
Industrial Revolution that there was not room for tiresome natural features
which got in the way of building a new mill or warehouse or laying a new
road. To 19th-century engineers the answer was to culvert any river, stream,
brook or canal which threatened to curtail building development activities. It
did not seem to be a great loss. Such was the pollution of these waterways by
industrial and domestic effluent that many were little more than open sewers
and some were even poisonous. Most waterways, though, great or small,

*Pavement proverb etching
in Tib Street.*

The Waterhouse pub and restaurant built over the culverted River Tib which flows beneath the basement.

Part of the Artworks from Gasworks project on Whitworth Street West near Gaythorn and Deansgate Station, below and opposite page.

usually saw daylight again at some point. However, in the case of the unfortunate River Tib, this was not to be the case, and it was culverted, diverted and enclosed to the extent that the river was, to all intents and purposes, 'buried alive'.

The first Rolls-Royce car,
1907. (Manchester
Archives & Local Studies,
Central Library)

In Roman times the Tib marked the limits of the Roman *vicus*, or settlement, and, according to popular legend, was given its name by homesick Roman soldiers who called it the Tib after the Tiber; shortening its name to mark the difference in size of the two rivers. However, 'tib' derives from a Celtic term meaning 'watercourse', so the Romans may have just been indulging in simple word play. The Tib continued to mark the town boundary until mediaeval times and it also supplied the population with drinking water. The river rose in a spring called Cooper's Pit at Miles Platting and flowed through the town to join the Medlock at Gaythorn Gas Works, close to Knotts Mill on Deansgate. Old machinery from the Gas Works has been used as part of an 'Artworks from Gasworks' project. Improbable looking 'Heath Robinson' mechanical items have been gaily painted in polite graffiti style and arranged under the arches that carry the line from Piccadilly through Oxford Road alongside Whitworth Street West to Deansgate Station (Knott Mill) and beyond.

The river approached the town via what is now Oldham Road and then crossed Swan Street, in the Northern Quarter, to flow down Tib Street into the city centre. Just before Market Street an old coaching inn, the Bridgewater Arms, stood on Tib Street opposite the river, on a site covered by the former Rylands warehouse, built in 1930 of Portland stone, and now Debenhams department store. The Bridgewater Arms was where the Manchester Mechanics Institute, which later became UMIST, was founded at a public meeting in 1823. Robert Southey mentions the inn in his *Letters,* published in 1808, as '...a spacious inn, the Bridgewater Arms.' and de Quincey left the inn to set out on a ride which he later commemorated in *The English Mail Coach*. The Bridgewater Arms acted as an unofficial mail depot for the letters and packets carried in bags on the stagecoaches until January 1816 when there was a robbery and the mail from several northern towns and cities was stolen as the guard was dealing with the London mail bags.

It is recorded that in Tudor times fustian dyers had their crofts alongside the river in what is now Tib Street. By the mid-18th century the Tib had flags across at the point where it emerged in Market Street, now beneath Starbucks coffee shop, and crossed to flow underneath the former Lewis's building, which currently houses McDonalds and T.K. Maxx, towards Spring Gardens. Ogden talks of the Tib being already culverted in this area in 1788; but in 1794 it was still open at St Peter's Fields and the point where it entered the Medlock at Gaythorn via a dismal channel through the early millscapes.

An earlier description comes from Ogden, which gives some idea of the Tib and its surrounding area when the river was still visible:

> *...the Tib once had a cluster of pleasant homesteads along its unculverted banks...this was Labery's Ffould sometimes called ye Labery's Houses which stood nearly upon the spot where York Street crosses Moseley Street, but beneath the present surface level...*

The Tib then flows underground down West Mosley Street, along Cooper Street, crosses Princess Street to Lloyd Street, flows under the Town Hall extension and the rear of Central Library (which is why the storage rooms in the basement are occasionally liable to flood), across Peter Street and beneath a corner of the Midland Hotel's smart dining room, under the Metrolink tracks on Lower Mosley Street, down Bale Street and heads for Gaythorn. There is a record that this section was culverted in 1820, the year after Peterloo. The Waterhouse, a Wetherspoon public house where good cheap lunches can be had, stands on the corner of Cooper Street and Princess Street and its name may commemorate the Tib that flows beneath it.

The Midland Hotel is celebrating the centenary this year (2004) of the first meeting in May 1904 of Frederick Royce, an electrical engineer, and the Hon. Charles Rolls, at the hotel. As a result of this meeting the first Rolls-Royce motor car was born in a Hulme back street in 1905. By 1906 the company had established works in Cooke Street. A 10 horsepower car cost around £400 while a top-of-the-range 30 horsepower car sold for about £900. The two men lunched together in the Nico Restaurant at the Midland, excitedly discussing their proposed new joint venture, and completely unaware of the lost river flowing through the darkness a few feet beneath them.

Deansgate railway station, formerly the station for Knott Mill. The River Tib joined the River Medlock nearby.

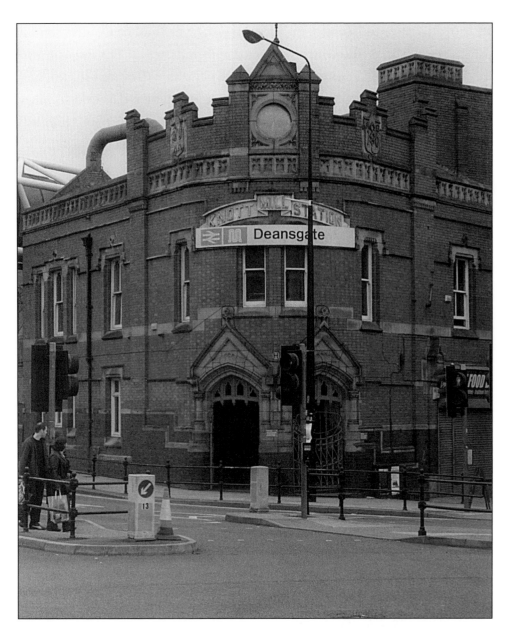

1820 probably marks the last time that the Tib saw daylight properly. Occasionally road works cut through the darkness, but otherwise it seems as if the Tib is destined to stay buried. It sounds as if it was a pretty river once and it is a shame that is now lost to view. Victorian engineers must have had great faith in their cobbled and culverted waterway tunnels, since it is practically impossible to check them today. Perhaps one day the Tib will make an impromptu reappearance.

A fitting epitaph to the River Tib may be a quotation etched, letter by letter, into small paving stones and set into a pavement on Tib Street:

> *where the water runs*
> *as the world defrosts*
> *the street breathes*
> *beneath this stone*

Saturday Nights and Music Hall

NO ACCOUNT of past, lost or hidden parts of the city would be complete without a picture of the people themselves, many of whom now lie in graveyards beneath the modern streets tramped by the feet of later generations coming out into the city for pretty much the same reasons as their forebears. Journalist Angus Bethune Reach tramped the Manchester streets of the 1840s, recording city life and one of the great lost institutions of the old industrial town, that of the Music Halls. His vivid pen portrait, written before the days of cameras, tape recorders, moving pictures and radio, is all that we have to show what early 19th-century Mancunian city life, now quite literally hidden from sight, was like:

...let me try to describe a curiously characteristic place of amusement which I visited the other day in Manchester. I was anxious to see and judge for myself one of the music saloons, of which I had heard so much; and so, ascertaining the Apollo in the London-Road [London-Road is the present A6 running from Piccadilly south through Ardwick to Stockport and beyond; but the Apollo mentioned here is not the same place as the rock concert venue of today] *presented a very good specimen. I waited until Saturday night should exhibit it in its greatest glory, then set off for the hall of jollity and harmony. The London-Road is full of cheap shops devoted to the sale of ordinary household matters. Stalls, covered and uncovered, heaped over with still coarser and cheaper wares, abound. Gas flares and blazes amid the joints in the butcher's open shops. Faintly burning candles, enclosed in greasy paper lanterns, cast their dim and tallowy influence over tables slimy with cheap fish, or costermongers' barrows littered with cabbages or apples. The gin shops are in full feather – their swinging doors never hang a moment still. Itinerant*

bands blow and bang their loudest; organ boys grind monotonously; ballad singers or flying stationers make roaring proclamations of their wares. The street is one swarming buzzing mass of people. Boys and girls shout and laugh and disappear into the taverns together. Careful housewives – often attended by their husbands, dutifully carrying the baby – bargain hard with the butchers for halfpenny off in the pound. In a cheap draper's shop, a committee of young women will be examining into the merits of a dress which one of them has determined to buy; while, in an underground pie-shop, a select party of juveniles will be regaling themselves upon musty pasties of pork. The pawnbroker is busy, for pledges are being rapidly redeemed, and flat irons, dirty pairs of stays, candlesticks, Sunday trousers, tools, blankets, and so forth, are fast being removed from his shelves. The baker has chalked on a black board... 'down again to even money – four pound loaf for five pence!' Here a woman is anxiously attempting half to drive half to lure home her drunken husband; there a couple of tipsy fellows are in high dispute, their tobacco pipes in their hands, and a noisy circle of backers urging them on...stalls, shops and cellars are clustered round with critics or purchasers...cabmen drive slowly through the throng, shouting and swearing to the people to get out of the horse's way; and occasionally...the melodious burst of a roaring chorus surging out of the open windows of the Apollo...a bright lamp...points out the entrance...there is a check-taker...and...a charge of twopence is made...entitling the bearer to twopennyworth of refreshments...a broad steep staircase [leads to] a long narrow room... my twopenny coupon entitled me to a tumbler of porter...the walls were covered with paper representing carved woodwork...midway on one side was a small bar, where the landlady was drawing ale and beer, the only liquors for which the house was licensed...along the length of the [room] ran narrow...tables with benches on either side...make it all but impossible for the female waiters to hand the malt liquor about...at the upper end...was a small stage...upon the stage was...a 'set scene' of a cottage and a landscape...beneath was an orchestra consisting of two or three fiddles and a pianoforte...of the audience two-thirds might be men; the others were women...several with babies at their breasts...when I entered, a man...was singing one of those really pretty airs which have of late gained such popular renown...the audience joined in the chorus...so that, just as I entered, nearly two hundred voices...were entreating Susanna not to cry for the minstrel who was 'going to Alabama with his banjo on his knee'...I...heard half a dozen songs and witnessed a couple of dances...the only female performer was a little girl about twelve, who sang a 'medley song', and danced a pas to correspond...a young man...dressed as a soldier, went through a sort of parody of the manual exercise, then swinging round, exhibited himself with a mask tied to the back of his head, and his 'rear' made up for the front of a theatrical sailor, in which character he performed a most energetic hornpipe...

St Ann's Church and the lost graves

LADY ANN BLAND, a daughter of the Mosley family, grew up at Hulme Hall, a beautiful early Tudor building standing on the banks of the Irwell. Hulme Hall was said to have 'unearthly guardians' conjured by the Dowager Lady Prestwich to safeguard her fortune during the Civil War (1642–51). Lady Bland, however, had no time for such stories. She loyally supported Queen Anne and, like her mother, she was low church and she worshipped at the Presbyterian chapel on Cross Street. In 1708 Lady Bland decided to build a new church for the town and petitioned Parliament. Permission was granted and in May 1709 she laid the corner stone in a large cornfield, known as Acres Field, where the harvest thanksgiving fair and the market were held. In July 1712 the church was consecrated and dedicated to St Ann, the name reflecting Lady Bland's own name and that of the Queen.

St Ann's Church and square, 1745, the year that Bonnie Prince Charlie marched into Manchester and into St Ann's Square. (Manchester Archives & Local Studies, Central Library)

By 1720 St Ann's Square had replaced much of Acres Field; most of the rest being given over to St Ann's churchyard. In 1738 John Wesley preached in St Ann's Church. Then, at the end of November 1745, Bonnie Prince Charlie rode into St Ann's Square on his triumphant march south to claim the English crown. The citizens affected to give him a warm welcome just in case this man was to be their future king; but, under a year later, after Bonnie Prince Charlie's defeat at the battle of Culloden Moor, the bells of St Ann's pealed out in rejoicing and Mancunians crowded into the church to give thanks for their deliverance.

Today there are no fields or countryside surrounding St Ann's. Even the churchyard has mostly disappeared under the buildings of the Industrial Revolution and 'Cottonopolis' which engulfed Manchester. The last burial in St Ann's churchyard was on 31 May 1854. As the pressure increased for building land in the city centre the gravestones were lowered to a foot below the level of the pavement, although the graves were left in situ, and the railings were removed in 1892.

St Ann's graveyard, 1913. (Manchester Archives & Local Studies, Central Library)

*St Ann's Church interior,
photographed in 1980.*
(Manchester Archives &
Local Studies, Central
Library)

A few gravestones, including those of the de Quincey family, remained on show but that was deemed insufficient memorial for one gentleman. Consequently there is a tablet (erected in 1983 by members of John Shaw's Club) on the north wall of the tower which gives precise directions for locating the grave of John Shaw, 'Master of the Punch House in the Shambles of this City', a convivial and popular 'mine host' of the 18th century.

Born in 1715, John Shaw opened his punch house in a 14th-century building which stood on the market place (the market place of 1738 is today occupied mainly by Marks & Spencer's new store). John Shaw also started the first gentleman's club in Manchester at his punch house, where he continued to live until his death on 26 January 1796. He was given an appropriately alcoholic send-off and according to the inscription on the tablet: '...his body lies five yards to the north and five feet to the west of the north-west corner of this tower...'

These directions can be paced out and the spot located quite easily, although doing so will attract some curious looks and perhaps even a cautious enquiry from the friendly neighbourhood police officer.

John Shaw would no doubt have thoroughly approved of the use of part of St Ann's former churchyard as a 'beer garden' for Mr Thomas's Chop House, a charismatic anachronism which has survived since the end of Queen Victoria's reign. Chairs and tables are arranged across the uneven flag stones and on warm summer afternoons the Chop House is a popular haunt for students and those who just want to relax with a long cool drink before sampling the culinary delights on offer. Some, who wish to engage in deep philosophical conversations, sit cross-legged on the few remaining tombstones against the east wall of the church, clutching their bottles of beer and talking earnestly among themselves. No one gives much thought to the neat rows of skeletons lying just a few feet beneath, or the fact that they too were once living people who talked and laughed and enjoyed a drink in the summer sunshine. Just a few yards away lies the most appropriately named shop in St Ann's Square: Past Times.

The Lost Canal

THE PROBLEM with old maps of Manchester is the lack of resemblance they bear to the modern city. The map makers cannot be blamed for that. The Industrial Revolution, the millscapes, the Blitz and latterly the IRA, have probably changed the face of Manchester more than any other city in England. Open fields have long since disappeared; picturesque timbered manor houses have either been pulled down or blown up; streams and rivers have been culverted; street names have changed or disappeared or moved location. So trying to find a canal of which there is virtually no trace today was never going to be easy.

Granby Row, where Vimto was created, seemed a good starting point since it was at least shown on the map of 1794 and it lay close to the supposed course of the lost canal. In 1794 Granby Row emerged onto Brook Street but Brook Street has moved south and today Granby Row actually comes out on Princess Street, opposite Asia House. On the corner of Granby Row, in 1794,

The lost canal entrance on the bend of the River Tib behind Asia House. The canal has silted up 10-12ft since it was built in 1787 by the Duke of Bridgewater.

an imposing and picturesque black and white timbered Tudor manor house called Garrat Hall, a former seat of the Trafford family, with 'numerous gables and tall chimneys', stood on the banks of Shooters Brook. The hall has long since gone but the name is commemorated by a rather non-descript 1960s public house. Despite its plain external appearance, the pub is said to sell excellent beer and is popular with the students of nearby UMIST.

On the south side of Asia House is Charles Street, marked in 1794 as one of a grid plan of newly laid out streets on the southern side of the wildly curving River Medlock. In 1794 Charles Street appears to have been pretty rural but this is far from the case today. At the point where the River Medlock passes under Charles Street bridge there is a red-brick pub, of typical Victorian appearance, with a brown tiled façade, called the Lass o'

The Lass o'Gowrie public house on Charles Street. The bridge over the River Medlock can be seen on the right. A urinal was built out over the river but was closed in 1896.

Gowrie. On one corner there is an information board which, for those who can read colloquial Scottish, will tell the story of Kitty who became 'Leddie Gowrie'. On the other corner by the bridge, fixed to the wall overlooking the Medlock, is a plaque which proudly proclaims:

> *Here was the site of*
> *Manchester's oldest*
> *Pissotière*
> *retained for*
> *Posterity*
> *Last used A.D. 1896*

As the wall on to which this sign is fixed drops straight down to the river and the waist high parapet of the bridge is flush with the wall, the potential problems of using this particular public urinal are best left to the imagination; or, in modern psycho-babble, 'don't go there'!

Behind the Lass o' Gowrie lies the Charles Street NCP car park. A friendly word with security in the cabin at the entrance is advisable to set minds at rest since finding the entrance to the lost canal can involve loitering with intent, hanging over riverside walls at odd angles and getting vicious with the brambles at the far end of the car park. The River Medlock curves round the car park at right angles. Walk straight across the car park from the entrance and peer over the bramble covered wall at the far end before the river curves round to flow under Charles Street. On the far side of the river at the foot of a high brick wall, just a few inches above the level of the water, is what appears to be the top of a curved archway.

The 'Duke's Tunnel', as the canal became known, ran directly from the Medlock, close to, or along, the course of Shooters Brook, to a coal wharf, close to the present Piccadilly railway station, on Shooters Brow (as it was named in 1794), now known as London Road. Shooters Brow was a steep bank leading down to the pretty Shooters Brook which ran through open fields full of snipe. It was originally called Snipe's Brook; the name was changed due to the prolific shooting of the unfortunate snipe. Willow trees and small country cottages and fishponds stood along the banks of the brook, which has long since been culverted under Whitworth Street. Today the dried up bed of Shooter's Brook is only visible for a short distance alongside the International Hotel and Monroes, opposite Piccadilly Station where the Metrolink emerges, before it disappears under London Road and along Store Street at a point which would have been between the steep slopes of Shooters Brow and Bank Top in 1794.

The Duke of Bridgewater built the canal in 1787, to run partly through an underground tunnel so that it could '...carry coal from the... Bridgewater Canal at Castlefield, along the Medlock and through the tunnel to a coal wharf...' (G. Ashworth, *The Lost Rivers of Manchester*, Willow Publishing, 1987). The coal wharf belonged to Knowles and Sons and the site can still be seen by walking down Station Approach from Piccadilly Station and turning sharp left at the bottom. On the pavement along London Road opposite Shepley Street there is a wide recess with high walls. The walls bear commemorative plaques to the workers of Manchester in the Industrial

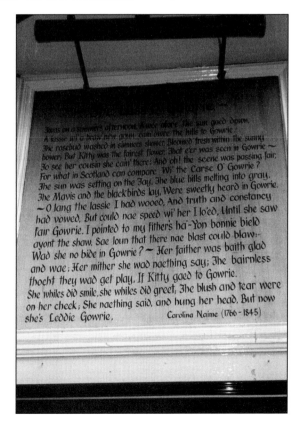

Plaque giving the legend of the Lass O'Gowrie.

Revolution, though these are mostly hidden by hanging fronds of green ivy. It is here that the lost canal emerged, bringing barges laden with coal from Castlefield Basin to the industrial heartland of the city.

Two 19th-century letters bear witness to the lost canal:

...between the Rochdale Canal and Shooters Brook lies deeply buried the now disused 'Duke's Tunnel'. Formerly coal boats ascended from the River Medlock to a wharf located near the junction of Ducie Street and London Road. The tunnel is still claimed (1879) by the trustees of the Duke as their property, possibly with an eye to its future value as an underground railway. The entrance from the Medlock into the tunnel was...apart from ...Shooters Brook but now one opening into (or from) the Medlock serves as both

The site of Manchester's oldest public urinal, last used in 1896. The plaque is on the wall of the Lass O'Gowrie pub on Charles Street.

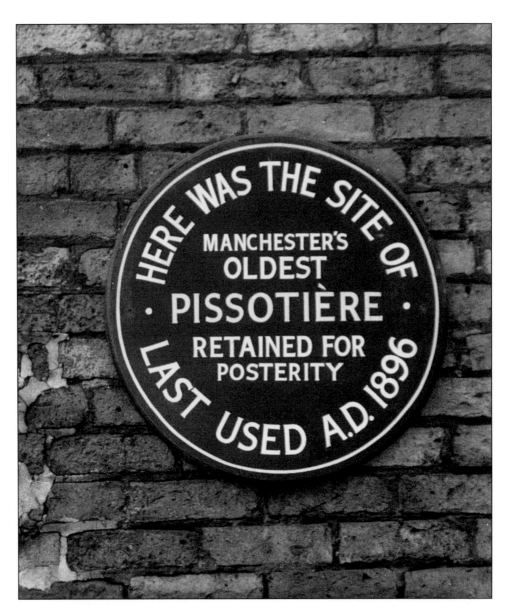

tunnel and brook. The brook and tunnel were very close together on the ground now covered by…Whitworth Street. There was a weir on the brook about there, and boys when bathing, were accustomed to pass (by an underwater opening) from the brook into the tunnel and bring out coal from a sunken boat…

[in 1874]…It is worth noting that a path in the waters has been lost to us by the silting up of the River Medlock;…[currently some eight or nine feet] … for filling up at the rate of one half an inch per year, it effectively stopped the means of supplying…coals in boats by water from Worsley along the Bridgewater Canal, then into the Medlock, and from thence by culvert upon the bosom of Shooter's Brook…

(G. Ashworth, The Lost Rivers of Manchester, Willow Publishing, 1987).

The Lowry

SALFORD QUAYS, once Manchester's waterfront gateway to the rest of the world, has reinvented itself completely for the 21st century and at the same time paid tribute to one of its most famous sons. L.S. Lowry, remembered for his paintings of the millscapes bustling with little stick-like people immortalised in the popular song *Matchstick Men*, has lent his name to an ambitious arts and heritage project which has completely transformed the 19th-century wharves and quays.

L.S. Lowry (1887–1976) was born in Rusholme and attended school in Victoria Park. Later he was a student at Manchester College of Art and Salford School of Art. He lived in Salford for 40 years but he also worked in Manchester, Stockport and Mottram-in-Longdendale. In 1945 he was awarded an honorary MA from Manchester University and he became a member of the Royal Academy in 1962. He eventually moved to Mottram-in-Longdendale and it was there that he died in 1976.

The workmen who painstakingly built the Manchester Ship Canal in 1894, to connect Manchester to the world, would not recognise the place. The dock basins have been cleaned and filled with fish. There are angling clubs and water sports. Most of the craft on the canal now are river boats or small cruise ships. Gone are the big transatlantic or international steam ships, the docks, the carriers, the cargoes just unloaded or waiting to be loaded, the warehouses full of cotton bales, the rows of steam locomotives waiting to be shipped all over the world. Replacing them is 'an architectural flagship', the 'National Landmark Millennium Project for the Arts', which is designed to be 'a unique centre for creativity bringing together…performing and visual arts…'. Mr Lowry would surely have approved.

The Lowry Project is situated in the area of the former No.9 Dock, opened by King Edward VII and Queen Alexandra in 1905. The docks closed in 1982 and The Lowry was formally opened in 2000 by Edward VII's great-granddaughter, Queen Elizabeth II, and her husband the Duke of Edinburgh. The Lowry includes two theatres: the Lyric Theatre and the Quays Theatre; galleries which display the works of L.S. Lowry and other contemporary artists; Artworks (a creative community project); bars, cafés, two shops and a waterside restaurant. The Lowry Project also includes the Plaza, a shopping centre, the Digital World Centre, a unique lifting footbridge across the Manchester Ship Canal, and the Imperial War Museum North. All this, however, is simply known to everyone as The Lowry.

On one side of the Plaza are restaurants and coffee shops where the emphasis is on alfresco eating. Sitting in the sunshine under the gaily coloured awnings, sipping cappuccino, watching the world and the river flow by, it is easy to forget that this is Manchester and not a Continental city like Venice, Paris or Milan. French markets are held regularly in the Plaza – genuine French markets – so it helps to take a French phrase book along since some of the traders speak little English. Sometimes the footbridge parts and lifts with the help of huge hydraulic machinery, to allow a larger than usual vessel to pass beneath. Across the bridge, on the Trafford wharfside, there is easy access to Manchester United's Old Trafford football ground and Lancashire County Cricket Club; and there is the Imperial War Museum North standing by the waterside.

The Imperial War Museum North is an unusual and unique experience (to which entrance is free); especially for those of us who have never known war at first hand. It is not a conventional museum. It tells the story of 'how war has shaped people's lives since 1900'. The designer, Daniel Libeskind, described his aims:

> *...the building has been created out of three shards or pieces of a shattered globe to reflect the way war has devastated our world. The air, earth and water shards represent war in the air on land and at sea...*

The Air Shard has a '55m high tower which leans at 4 degrees' and offers stunning views over Manchester. There is also a Harrier jump-jet on show. The Water Shard overlooks the canal and includes a restaurant. The Land Shard is the largest shard and the one which demands attention.

There are six time lines: 1900–14; 1914–18; 1919–38; 1939–45; 1946–90; 1990–present; and half a dozen 'silos' with special exhibitions including: experience of war; women and war; impressions of war; Empire, Commonwealth and war; science, technology and war; and legacy of war. Rounding the Impressions of War silo, one comes unexpectedly face to face with a real Russian tank. It is a startling and sobering moment. The showpiece highlights of the museum, however, are its three Big Picture Shows: *Why War?*; *Weapons of War*; *Children and War*. To quote:

> *...the Big Picture is a large-scale audio-visual experience that you can walk through... it uses over sixty projectors throwing images onto twenty screens, some of them five meters high, and has a powerful soundtrack of personal stories...*

As a result the audience is surrounded by the noise, scenes, drama and the

tragedy of war. There is no
longer a museum or screens with
seats like in a cinema; this a 3D
interpretation of war as it is and
was. You are in the middle of
battle, the Blitz, a field of
poppies, women talking, the
Home Guard clearing a bombed
street, children wearing gas
masks... It can be over-
whelming, frightening and
fascinating in turn. The whine of

*The Imperial War
Museum North standing
beside the Manchester
Ship Canal opposite the
Lowry Centre.*

the air-raid sirens, the roar of the planes, the sound of gunfire is all around
you. Fire watchers on night duty stand on roofs of buildings to see where the
bombs fall, desperately hoping that they won't fall on their building or in
their street. This writer's mother was a fire watcher in Manchester during
World War Two and, although she described her experiences quite
graphically, it has not been possible until now to understand what she
actually endured, and at an age at which most early 21st-century girls expect
to be carefree and spending their spare time in pubs, clubs and cinemas.

Suddenly there is silence. The show has ended. Many of the audience are
emotionally exhausted. They have seen more, heard more and learned more
about war and what it really means in the last 15 minutes than, hopefully, most
of them will experience in their lifetimes. Personal perspectives have altered.
The Imperial War Museum North proclaims itself 'a war museum with a heart'
and it is. It reaches the parts that other static museums often cannot; and it will
touch the hearts of those who enter with an unforgettable experience.

*The Digital World Centre
and the unique lifting
footbridge across the
Manchester Ship Canal are
part of the Lowry
complex.*

The Triangle

T HE FORMER Corn and Produce Exchange, now the Triangle shopping
centre, was built in the 19th century along Hanging Ditch over the
culverted River Dene, probably close to the site of a tithe barn where local
tenants' grain payments would have been collected after the milling of their
corn at the nearby corn mill.

*The Corn Exchange
building, photographed in
1900.* (Manchester
Archives & Local Studies,
Central Library)

*The interior of the Corn
Exchange, 1902.*
(Manchester Archives &
Local Studies, Central
Library)

*...there is the mill of Mamcestre running by the water of the Irk... to
which all the burgesses and all the tenants of the town of Mamcestre
with hamlets of Ardwicke, Oponshaghe* [Openshaw], *Curmesalle*
[Crumpsall], *Moston, Nuthurst... and Ancottes ought to grind their
grain to the sixteenth grain...*[some to be left behind as payment for
the miller]...

    (*Survey of the Manor of Manchester,* 1322)

The mill stood perhaps at the site of Mill Brow, shown on Green's map
of 1794, leading from the banks of the Irk to Long Millgate. This corn

The Triangle, formerly the Corn and Produce Exchange, 2003. A corn mill used to stand near this spot.

mill may not have been the first corn mill, however. An earlier survey in 1282 mentions two water-driven corn mills and it is thought that the first mill may have been built around 930 and stood on the former River Dene at Old Millgate, a street which stood on the site of the steps up to Exchange Square opposite the Old Wellington Inn, leading to the former site of the Old Shambles. Old Millgate is shown clearly on Green's map of 1794. This supposition is further strengthened by the fact that during building work in Cateaton Street during the early 19th century '...a bed or mass of shudes or shells of oats, quite black – there were cartloads of these shudes...' (J. Reilly, *A History of Manchester*) was discovered at a depth of several feet.

The architecture of this unusual triangular corn exchange is imposing and was designed to reflect the growing importance and status of Manchester during the era of 'Cottonopolis'. The green and white tiled Victorian entrance has been preserved together with dizzying flights of stairs around a central stairwell which rises about six storeys high.

The interior has been converted into an upmarket shopping centre with three floors of designer shops and cafés, and lots of deep purple sofas and easy chairs on which to relax. The glass sides of the escalators allow views of the rotating working wheels; an oblique reference to the engineering feats of the Industrial Revolution; and there is a circular glass lift in one corner.

However, despite the creative effort and vision which has been put into this conversion, and the brave attempts to reflect something of the city's history, the Corn and Produce Exchange will not give up its identity easily. There is somehow still the feeling that the old building would be more at home with corn and potato merchants still making their deals below the tattered posters for Birds custard powder on the walls. It has yet to come to terms with the tastes of its 21st-century customers for crafts, clothes, cappuccino and 'chilling'.

Outside though, the Triangle has met with more success. A large BBC screen is fixed to the outside wall and gives constant news and sports coverage. People stop to watch, or sit and listen on the wide semi-circular terrace of stone steps which sweeps round in an arc in front of Selfridges and Harvey Nichols, facing the old mediaeval heart of the city: the Cathedral, the culverted Hanging Ditch and the lost River Dene, the Old Wellington Inn, Sinclair's (John Shaw's former punch house), the old corn mill and produce market. Fountains of water rise from pavement panels. It is an ideal meeting place to gossip, to chill, to just feel a part of the scene, and that always was a major function of the former Corn Exchange: to meet, to gossip, to be a part of the scene, as well as to trade produce.

Victoria Station and what it hides

MUCH OF Victoria Station in Manchester has remained unaltered since Victorian times. Originally known as Hunts Bank Station, it was first opened in 1842. Today it is managed by First North Western and is used mainly by cross-Pennine services to Harrogate, Leeds, York and Bradford. The brown and white Victorian tiles and the old wooden Victorian ticket office are still features. So too are the façades of the former 1st Class Refreshment Room, the 1st Class restaurant and the Grill Room. The former bookstall is now the Northern Belle, which is the Manchester venue for the Orient Express, where tickets can be booked and passengers collected.

Outside the station the glass canopy still proclaims that trains for Leeds, Harrogate, Bradford, York, Scarborough, Newcastle, Hull, Belgium, Liverpool, Southport, Blackpool, Fleetwood, Goole, Ireland, Scotland and London will depart from the station. An interesting and varied choice of destinations. The Bury-bound Metrolink also uses the station, swooping down from Balloon Street where a statue of Robert Owen stands at the junction with Long Millgate. In the 1830s and 1840s Robert Owen fought to reduce children's working hours in the mills.

The interior of Victoria Station, 1988. (Manchester Archives & Local Studies, Central Library)

Today it is hard to recognise Friedrich Engels's description of the Victoria Station and Hunts Bank areas in 1842; especially as Long Millgate now only refers to a short street which runs along the side of Victoria Station. In 1794 Miller Street and Swan Street were also part of Long Millgate; while the present Victoria Street was called Hunts Bank; and the River Irk is now partly culverted and runs beneath the northern perimeter of Victoria and the Nynex Arena.

...this sketch will be sufficient to illustrate the crazy layout of the whole district lying near the River Irk. There is a very sharp drop of some 15 to 30 feet down to the south bank of the Irk at this point. As many as three rows of houses have generally been squeezed onto this precipitous slope. The lowest row of houses stands directly on the bank of the river while the front walls of the highest row stand on the crest of the ridge in Long Millgate. Moreover, factory buildings are also to be found on the banks of the river. In short the layout of the upper part of Long Millgate at the top of the rise is just as disorderly and congested as the lower part of the street. To the right and left a number of covered passages from Long Millgate give access to several courts. On reaching them one meets with a degree of dirt and revolting filth the like of which is not to be found elsewhere. The worst courts are those leading down to the Irk, which contain unquestionably the most dreadful dwellings I have ever seen. In one of these courts, just at the entrance where the covered passage ends, there is a privy without a door. This privy is so dirty that the inhabitants of the court can only enter or leave the court if they are prepared to wade through puddles of stale urine and excrement. Anyone who wishes to confirm this description should go to the first court on the bank of the Irk above Ducie Bridge. Several tanneries are situated on the bank of the river and they fill the neighbourhood with the stench of animal putrefaction. The only way of getting to the courts below Ducie Bridge is by going down flights of narrow dirty steps and one can only reach the houses by treading over heaps of dirt and filth. The first court below Ducie Bridge is called Allen's Court. At the time of the cholera [1832] this court was in such a disgraceful state that the sanitary inspectors [of the local Board of Health] evacuated the inhabitants. The court was then swept and fumigated with chlorine...

(Friedrich Engels, *Condition of the Working Classes in England*, 1844)

Vimto

GOING DOWN the escalators and coming out of the new ground floor entrance of Piccadilly railway station brings one out onto London Road opposite Granby Row. Like its name, Granby Row does not appear anything special; just another road left over from the millscapes with tall buildings on either side which might once have been warehouses. Appearances, however, can be deceptive.

Today much of the north side of Granby Row is taken up with new residential blocks for students at UMIST. The two most prominent warehouses still standing are Granby House and Orient House down at the far end towards Princess Street. The south side of the street midway down is given to a large grassy area, owned by UMIST, that stretches as far the railway arches which shield the academic buildings of UMIST from view.

In 1908 Granby Row was a busy, well-populated street. There were two churches, two inns, public dining rooms and a host of small manufacturers. No.49 lay on the south side of the Row, not far from Sackville Street. It was occupied by T. Shackleton and Co. who were manufacturing stationers. By late 1908, however, T. Shackleton must either have suffered a decline in fortunes or simply needed help with the rent, for they let out the top floor of the building to J.N. Nichols and Co. who were wholesale druggists. It was a momentous decision for in 1908 John Noel Nichols created a new drink called Vimto.

Vimto was made to a secret herbal recipe as a 'health tonic' that people could drink to gain 'vim and vigour', hence the name. The drink was a rich fruity cordial to which hot, cold or carbonated water was added. Two years later the company had greatly expanded and moved across the River Irk to No.203 Chapel Street in Salford, close to the centre of Manchester. At first Vimto was sold in herbalists and temperance bars in Manchester, but it rapidly gained in popularity and today it is known worldwide. The original cordial is still very popular, either as a hot or a cold drink, while Vimto Light and sparkling Vimto in cans are also available. John Noel Nichols died in 1966 but his grandsons still run the company.

*A light dusting of snow
lies on the Vimto
monument marking the
site of 49 Granby Row,
where Vimto was first
produced to a secret recipe
in 1908.*

No.49 Granby Row no longer exists so in 1992 it was decided, with the agreement of UMIST, that a Vimto monument should commemorate the site of the original premises, the place where it all began. A wooden monument was designed by sculptor Kerry Morrison and completed in July 1992, when it was unveiled by *Coronation Street* actress Rita Sullivan. The oak sculpture stands on the grassy area between the UMIST residential block and the railway arches. It consists of a large wooden Vimto bottle surrounded by wooden models of raspberries, blackcurrants and herbs used in the making of the drink; the whole resting on a stone tray. The early morning sun catches the bottle and gives the wood a deep rich golden sheen. In winter this is highlighted when there is a light dusting of snow on the ground. This little oasis of green grass, with its unexpected and unusual commemoration of Vimto, is well known to UMIST students but often missed by visitors to the city.

Eyewitness in Manchester before 1900

THE EYEWITNESS accounts of a Manchester that is now lost, or, should one say, permanently hidden, are just as fascinating as any of the unknown corners of the city. The city will never again be just a small market town standing in pretty wooded countryside at a point where three rivers meet, a trading centre for the surrounding picturesque country villages. It has changed more quickly and more irrevocably than most towns and cities.

> *...the fairest, best buildid, quikkest and most populous tounne of all Lancastreshire...on Hirke [Irk] river be divers faire mills...*
> (John Leland, *Itinerary* 1540)

> *...there is a large church, all stone, and standeth so high that, walking around the church yard you see the whole town...*
> (Celia Fiennes, visiting in 1697)

> *...Manchester... the largest, most rich, populous, and busy village in England having about 2,400 families... they have looms which work twenty four laces at once, which were stolen from the Dutch...*
> (William Stukely, *Itinerarium Curiosum* 1724)

> *The dwellings of the labouring manufacturers are in narrow streets and lanes, blocked up from light and air... crowded together because every inch of land is of such value, that room for light and air cannot be afforded them... the houses all built of brick and blackened with smoke; frequent buildings among them as large as convents, without*

their antiquity, without their beauty, without their holiness; where
you hear from within...the everlasting din of machinery...
    (Robert Southey 1774–1843)

A couple of miles north of the city centre, Collyhurst, later given over to dyeing and chemical works, was a completely different place in 1800.

...the carriageway [to Collyhurst Hall] *was through an avenue of trees to Miles Platting... about the Hall itself... there was thick woodland... one or two meadows stretched beyond the boundary in the direction of the coal pit... when Tinker's Gardens flourished* [there were] *wild flowers and blackberries on the banks of Moss Brook... and... honeysuckle... while overhead the wild birds sung as gaily as if they were in the groves of paradise...*
    (P. Wentworth, *Middleton Guardian*, February 1887)

However by 1835 Alexis de Toqueville could write of Manchester:

...the greatest stream of human industry flows out to fertilise the whole world... from this filthy sewer pure gold flows... here humanity attains its most complete development and its most brutish; here civilisation works its miracles, and civilised man is turned back into savage...

Samuel Bamford, an early 19th-century Manchester mill worker and poet, who was one of the speakers at Peterloo, wrote of his home in Moston around 1840:

The knight he rode east, t'wards the uprising sun, but the broad heaths of Moston [Manchester] *lay silent and dun...*
    (Samuel Bamford, *The Wild Rider of Lancashire. c.*1840)

W. Cooke Taylor undertook a tour of Lancashire in 1842 and recorded what he saw:

...I remember my earliest view of Manchester, when I looked upon the town for the first time and saw the forest of chimneys pouring forth volumes of steam and smoke, forming an inky canopy which seemed to embrace and involve the entire place...
    (W. Cooke Taylor, *Notes of a Tour of the Manufacturing Districts*
    of Lancashire, 1842)

Friedrich Engels, who spent some time in Manchester in the middle of the 19th century, 'field walked' the city's millscapes.

> *...on the left side of the Medlock lies Hulme which...is one great working people's district... [and] southward from Great Ancoats Street lies a great straggling working men's quarter... occupied by... rows of houses or squares...*
> (Friedrich Engels, *Condition of the Working Class in England,* 1845)

Manchester was one of the places the children's writer, Beatrix Potter, had most wanted to visit and she was overjoyed when her wish was finally granted in 1883. She writes in her *Journal* how she saw the house in Greenheys (near Oxford Road) where her father had been born; the neighbouring suburb of Rusholme which was still green fields; Owen's College, which stood on the site of the house where her Uncle Crompton was born, is now part of Manchester University; the textile warehouses of her grandfather and uncles in Mosley Street, Charlotte Street and Pall Mall in the city centre, and Aunt Harriet's house in Fallowfield. Beatrix did not visit places like Ancoats and Chorlton-on-Medlock and Hulme. The only features she would still be able to recognise from what she saw are the family warehouses on Mosley Street and Charlotte Street.

Warehouse City

MANCHESTER city centre, the heart of the trading empire, was where the inspection of wares, the buying and selling and money making was done. '...merchants used to live in the city but not since about 1825. Gone are their gracious houses for they were not large enough...'. The merchants now had so much cotton to sell that they could not store it in their houses so they built huge warehouses, between five and seven storeys high, around the city centre. The merchants themselves then moved out to live in the more 'genteel' districts of Cheetham Hill and Ardwick Green.

> *...Market Street is always busy, noisy, and interesting, and contains numbers of splendid shops. In the evening its thousands of gas-lights glittering from the shops and street lamps make it almost painfully dazzling to eyes not yet accustomed to these nightly illuminations of the great English cities... let us now turn into one of the by-streets which diverge from Market Street, into Mosley Street, or Cooper Street, for instance. Here stand the great warehouses, five or six storeys high, all large and imposing, some of them stately and elegant. At night these warehouses are brilliantly lighted from top to bottom...*
>
> (Johann Georg Kohl, 1844)

The Manchester Cotton Exchange was responsible for helping to create a world-wide market for its commodities. The first Cotton Exchange in Manchester was built in 1729 when it would have traded mostly in chintzes and printed calicoes. Subsequent rebuilding and enlargement of the Exchange took place and it later received a royal warrant from Queen Victoria, becoming known as the Manchester Royal Exchange.

The present Royal Exchange on Exchange Street was built 1914–21 and is the fourth Exchange built on the same site. The Exchange closed in 1968 but the final trading figures were left in situ as a memorial to the part cotton had played in the city's fortunes. Today the Royal Exchange building houses a

The doorway of the Royal Exchange building as it looked in 1972. (Manchester Archives & Local Studies, Central Library)

The last day's cotton trading figures, left in place when the Exchange closed in 1968. (Manchester Archives & Local Studies, Central Library)

'theatre in the round', a glass and steel structure built within the Exchange on the model of an Elizabethan circular playhouse. There is also a theatre café bar and a bookshop.

> *Manchester may be roughly divided into three great regions. The central of these – laying around the heart of the Exchange – is the grand district of warehouses and counting rooms. There the fabrics spun, wove, printed and dyed at the mills are stored for inspection and purchase. There the actual business of buying and selling is carried on. There are banks, offices agencies innumerable...*
> (*Manchester and the Textile Districts in 1849*, Angus Bethune Reach. Aspin, 1972, Helmshore Local History Society)

During the 19th century a number of large, architecturally ornate, home trade, import and export warehouses were built centred mainly around an area bound by Aytoun Street, Whitworth Street, Portland Street and Oxford Street. The principal 'warehouse streets' were Mosley Street, Portland Street and Princess Street. Warehouses were usually five or six storeys high with rows of well proportioned windows to allow in plenty of light in order that clients could see clearly the wares on offer. There are carriers warehouses, commercial warehouses and canal warehouses. The sheer number of warehouses built in such a comparatively small area has made the city centre of Manchester unique and distinctive. Amazingly most of these warehouses

Joshua Hoyle's former warehouse, which became the Malmaison Hotel, photographed in 1940. (Manchester Archives & Local Studies, Central Library)

survived and many have been regenerated, refurbished and reused.

On London Road, opposite the foot of Piccadilly Station Approach, is the former warehouse of Joshua Hoyle and Sons. A steel framed warehouse, encased in sandstone and terracotta, it was built alongside the Rochdale Canal in 1904 by Charles Heathcote. After the end of 'Cottonopolis', the warehouse fell into general disuse for a number of years. For a while, during the 1970s and early 1980s, there was a Dolls' Hospital in the end wing farthest from Station Approach. Treasured dolls were lovingly repaired and restored for both children and adults. Today the Malmaison Hotel occupies the building and luxury bedrooms have replaced the former 'hospital'. The hotel opened in 1998 with an emphasis on French décor, French comfort and French cuisine.

On Portland Street, facing Piccadilly Gardens, is a former warehouse building which used to be the Portland Hotel and before that the Queens Hotel. It now houses the Thistle Hotel plus the headquarters of the GMPTE (Greater Manchester Passenger Transport Executive). It was designed by Sir Edward Walters (who also designed the Free Trade Hall on Peter Street) in 1854 with an arcading façade and included Nos 3,5,7 and 9 Portland Street. The warehouse was owned by Kershaw, Leese and Sidebottom, merchants who were joined as owners in 1858 by James Brown and Co., merchants. In 1855 No.3 was occupied by Robert Barbour and Brother, Merchants; No.5 by Wright, Parlowe & Co., and Finnie Brothers & Co., both merchant

The interior of S. and J. Watts's textile trading emporium, 1960. (Manchester Archives & Local Studies, Central Library)

companies; and No.7 by Richard Evans, a metal merchant. Despite all the different names and different occupants the warehouse came to be known as Brown's Warehouse.

A little way down Portland Street on the same side is possibly the best known of all Manchester's warehouses; that of S. & J. Watts, which is now the Britannia Hotel. It was designed in the 1850s by Travis and Mangall. The building was six storeys high and each storey was of a different architectural style but all with a marine element, presumably to reflect Watts's international textile trade with ships sailing all over the world. Watts owned the largest wholesale drapery business in Manchester. Their first premises were in Deansgate, which they sold to Kendal Milne before moving to warehouses in New Brown Street and Fountain Street and then Portland Street. James Watts was knighted by Queen Victoria and twice became Mayor of Manchester.

The interior followed the typical warehouse layout of the day. Sample rooms were on the upper floors reached by a central staircase; offices and a showroom were on the ground floor, and the packing department was in the basement. The internal loading bays were known as 'hovels'; the wall cranes as 'teagles'.

Mosley Street, lined with elegant 18th-century houses, used to be one of the most fashionable streets in Manchester. They were the merchants' houses from which they conducted their business. Sadly, as the textile industry mushroomed, these were all demolished so that warehouses could be built while the merchants moved out to live in the suburbs. From 1825–40, warehouses were simple and functional in design. After 1840, with trade still booming, merchants sought to affirm their status and success through more impressive premises. It was at this point that the Italian 'palazzo' style became popular, inspired by the beautiful Renaissance architecture of Florence and Venice. The first Manchester warehouse in this style was designed by Edward Walters and built by Richard Cobden on Mosley Street in 1839.

Cobden, who was involved in politics and the Anti Corn Law League, neglected his business interests and he suffered financially. His friend and colleague, Edmund Potter, grandfather of the internationally acclaimed children's writer, Beatrix Potter, took over the warehouse for his rapidly growing business in printed calicoes. This warehouse survived and is today home to Lloyds TSB Bank at 14–16 Mosley Street. Potter also had a warehouse on Charlotte Street, at No.10 (not far from the Portico Library), which today houses Gibbs Bookshop in the old packing basement. There was another Italian 'palazzo' style warehouse built in 1856 at No.36 Charlotte Street (on the corner with Portman Street), which was also designed by Edward Walters.

S. and J. Watts's 'marine' exterior, Portland Street, 1970. (Manchester Archives & Local Studies, Central Library)

The palazzo-style warehouse built by Richard Cobden on Mosley Street and formerly owned by Edmund Potter of Dinting Vale.

Princess Street has an interesting collection of warehouses, the origins of which are unmistakable although most are used for other functions today. These include Asia House (No.82, at the back of which the opening for the Duke of Bridgewater's 'lost' canal can still just be seen); the adjacent Lancaster House (No.80); a warehouse (at No.74) that looks like a grand Transylvanian castle but which was designed in the 'Scottish Baronial' style in 1880; another palazzo-style warehouse (No.109); the People's History Museum at No.103 and the former 'Pickles Building' at No.101. The museum library is open to the public and contains the archives and history of working people and trade unions in Britain. The museum galleries can be viewed at the nearby Pump House, a former Edwardian hydraulic pumping station on Bridge Street.

The warehouses on the part of Whitworth Street between Princess Street and Oxford Road are large and close packed so as to be quite claustrophobic. Two of the largest are India House and Bridgewater House, which is home to a number of organisations including the British Council. Other warehouses of note in the city centre include Tootal, Broadhurst and Lee, built in 1896 at 56 Oxford Street; the Great Northern Railway Warehouse, now a block of shops, offices and cafés, in the right angle between Deansgate and Peter Street; a bonded warehouse, on Quay Street off Deansgate, which currently houses the Granada Television Studios; and the Liverpool Road Station Warehouse, the first railway warehouse in the world, built in 1830, which is now part of the Museum of Science and Industry.

One of the oldest warehouses is the Dale Warehouse in the Piccadilly Basin on the Rochdale Canal close to the junction with the Ashton Canal. A four-storey stone warehouse built in 1806, it actually looks much older. The arches where narrowboats and horse-drawn wagons entered are clearly visible. Goods doors and hoists can also be seen. Jacksons Warehouse is like a more up-to-date model of Dale Warehouse and was built on adjoining Tariff Street in 1836. These older canal warehouses, now a little hidden away, give much more idea of the function of warehouses and how this was achieved than those warehouses whose identity and purpose have been changed.

What lies beneath

THE FACE of Manchester has changed so much over the last couple of centuries; like someone turning a giant kaleidoscope around. Industrial and housing suburbs cover farms and fields and villages; rivers and canals are culverted; schools and churches are built, used and demolished; wars and Blitzes and terrorist bombs cause destruction, and then there are regeneration schemes which change the landscape yet again. The ground level is rising all the time as a result of natural sedimenting and detritus plus rebuilding and reusing sites. Present ground levels tend to be about a foot or two higher than in the mediaeval period; maybe up to four feet higher than in Roman times. Archaeologists will dig down through the layers to discover the features and artefacts of bygone ages, but they can only uncover a fraction of the land and its history. So what does lie beneath?

In Manchester much of the answer is starkly simple. Bodies. In 1543 the population of Manchester was just over 2,000; maybe 2,300 – smaller than many modern villages. Within the next two centuries it multiplied almost 20 times to more than 43,000 and the town quadrupled in size between 1660 and 1760. The population figures then exploded with the advent of the Industrial Revolution and the coming of 'Cottonopolis'. In 1801 the population was 322,000, nearly eight times larger than in 1773. This tripled to over a million in the next half century and then doubled again to 2.1 million by 1901. Everyone who is born has to die at some point. In Cottonopolis it was often sooner rather than later as typhoid, cholera, dysentery and tuberculosis ravaged the population in turn during the 19th century.

There were more churches and chapels in 19th-century Manchester than today but by the 1830s even they were fast running out of room for burials. In 1837 the first of Manchester's municipal cemeteries, which catered for burials from all denominations, was opened in Harpurhey. This relieved the pressure on the parish graveyards, many of which did not accept any more burials. The 20th century, however, brought the decline of Cottonopolis, a shift in industrial emphasis, two major wars and a redistribution of a population which was inclined less and less to actively practise religion. Many churches did not survive; and most of those that didn't were demolished. What to do with the graveyards? Some were moved but sheer logistics meant that a number were left in situ and simply covered over.

In English folklore there is a tradition that when a person suddenly feels an involuntary shiver it is because someone has walked across their grave; even though they are not yet occupying it! Consequently most people, when exploring country churchyards or looking for a particular burial, mutter a silent apology to the dead for walking across their graves. In Manchester, certainly in the city centre area, it is hard to avoid walking across someone's grave because of the number of old and lost graveyards.

St Ann's Square and Exchange Street is the site of the oldest known graveyard. It is not known when it opened but it had closed by the 10th century. It would most likely have been the graveyard for the small parish church that preceded the 10th-century parish church of St Mary's which formerly stood on the site of the Cathedral. In early Christian times, as in pre-Christian times, it was the custom to bury the dead away from population sites, usually for simple reasons of hygiene. At least part of this graveyard may have been moved in 1712 when St Ann's Church was built; but the records aren't clear. St Ann's own graveyard covered the southern end of the square and it may have been this area which was cleared. The graves of those buried at St Ann's were left in situ; the gravestones lowered about a foot below the surface and the whole lot covered over. One or two important gravestones, like those of the de Quincey family, have been left standing against the church walls; and there is a plaque on the tower with instructions for finding the grave of John Shaw, one of the more popular incumbents of St Ann's graveyard. His grave lies a few yards to the north-west of the tower. The location, under the paving stones of a busy pedestrian shopping area, suggests that he and his long-dead neighbours get no more eternal peace than those buried on the opposite side of St Ann's beneath the 'beer garden' of Mr Thomas's Chop House.

The Cathedral yard burial ground, in use from the 12th century to 1819, is still there in situ; and so is the graveyard which lies beneath the Apple Market, a short stretch of which lies between the Cathedral and Chetham's, at the end of Fennel Street. This graveyard was of short lived duration (1767–88) and may have been intended as a temporary or emergency measure, and not as permanent. The same goes for the burial ground in Walker's Croft, a dismal lane behind Chetham's which leads to Victoria Station. This burial ground was in use from 1815–32 and is supposed to have been partially moved in 1844. Walker's Croft is not a pleasant place to linger today.

Cross Street Unitarian Chapel had its own burial ground which was used from around 1700 to about 1854. It is supposed to have been moved in 1995 but it is doubtful whether all of it would have been removed because of surrounding buildings.

The former burial ground of St James in nearby Charlotte Street, where Crompton Potter's former warehouse (now Gibbs Bookshop) stands, in use from approximately 1788–1854, was only partially moved in 1964. The graveyard of St Mary's Church (the Hidden Gem) in Mulberry Street remains in situ although mostly hidden under subsequent building works. That in Parsonage Gardens (off Blackfriars Lane which leads from Deansgate), close to the Law Courts, was used from about 1760–1854 and again is still in situ.

St Peter's Square stands in front of Central Library. On the other side of the Metrolink stop is a roughly oval shaped piece of land on which the Cenotaph stands at the Oxford Street end. St Peter's Church, at one time a well-used city centre church, stood on this site, fronting onto Oxford Street. The church was demolished very early in the 20th century but the graveyard was left in situ and remains so today. There is a photograph, dating from around 1953, of Sir Laurence Olivier and Vivien Leigh, on a visit to Manchester, walking across what would have been the back of St Peter's Church where the graveyard was situated.

Further south from St Peter's, after Oxford Street has become Oxford Road, the modern building of Manchester Metropolitan University library, known as the All Saints Building, stands adjacent to a pleasant recreational park where flowering cherry blossoms in springtime. This is the former site of All Saints Church which was built in 1820, partially destroyed by fire in 1850, bombed in 1940, and finally demolished in 1945. All Saints drinking fountain, an ornate Victorian creation, erected in 1896, stood just outside the

The Cathedral from Long Millgate, 1900. (Manchester Archives & Local Studies, Central Library)

Cross Street Unitarian Chapel, 1957.
(Manchester Archives & Local Studies, Central Library)

former church gates until 1982. The graveyard, so far as is known, was left in situ. In summer the area is popular with students for eating sandwich lunches, revising for exams, or just sitting chatting, blissfully unaware of what lies beneath them. Just outside the graveyard underground toilets were built in the 1950s. A somewhat spooky convenience, maybe, that is now closed; and the cheerful market stall holder who sells good bargain fruit and vegetables from a stall on the site is probably also blissfully unaware of what lies beneath.

Wythenshawe Hall

WYTHENSHAWE HALL, the original seat of the Tatton family, was built as a moated manor house in Tudor times by Robert Tatton. There may well have been a mediaeval building on the site previously. There are records of a chapel standing in the grounds until 1688 though nothing can be seen of it today. A wall with intricate painted plaster decoration in the Withdrawing Room commemorates the marriage of Robert Tatton to Dorothy Booth in 1539; and a huge wooden four-poster bed in which they may have slept stands in the same room.

A tale of tragedy and passion was played out at the hall during the Civil War. In 1642, on 22 November, Colonel Robert Dukinfield arrived in the area at the head of the Parliamentarian troops. His soldiers smashed the east window of Northenden Church and the Rector fled to take refuge in Ferry House, which stood on the banks of the River Mersey. The Roundheads then laid siege to Wythenshawe Hall. The Robert Tatton of that time was a staunch Royalist who defended his home against the Roundheads. There was a fierce battle and six of the Royalist supporters defending the hall were killed.

One of the dead was engaged to a local girl named Mary Webb. She was completely heartbroken over his death. After two months of trying to come to terms with her devastating loss she determined on revenge. She took a rifle and she set out to track down Captain Adams, the Roundhead officer who had led the siege of the hall. On 25 February 1643 she found him and shot him dead at point blank range. She made no attempt to escape the consequences of her actions. In her eyes justice had finally been done for her dead sweetheart.

Robert Tatton fled to Chester. The Parliamentarians confiscated the hall and drew up an inventory of its contents. Towards the end of the Civil War the hall was returned to Robert Tatton but only after payment of a large fine. For the next 300 years life at the hall was prosperous for the Tattons if quieter

than it had been. In 1747 William Tatton married Hester Egerton, the heiress to Tatton Park. Their son, William, changed his name to Egerton so that he could succeed to the Tatton Park estate. The library at Wythenshawe was added in the 1790s by Lewis Wyatt, who was employed by William Tatton; and the Tenants Hall was added during the 1860s. By the mid-1920s the estate possessed 2,500 acres of land.

Wythenshawe Hall was sold to Manchester Corporation in 1926. Most of the farmland was utilised to build the garden city of Wythenshawe, but Wythenshawe Hall and its park were preserved. It is an impressive black and white timbered multi-gabled building now used to house council offices and an art gallery. The hall also hosts conferences and weddings. There is a

community farm and a large horticultural centre in the grounds of Wythenshawe Park. The farm sells home-reared beef, lamb and pork to visitors. Herbs, fruit and alpines are grown while the 'Safari Walk' offers rather more exotic plants in the form of banana, pineapple, tea, coffee and rice. The hall and community farm are curious, if rather beautiful, anomalies in the middle of a suburban 'garden' city, where the garden aspects are no longer much in evidence and where the population now exceeds that of places like Cambridge.

Appendix

Manchester Visitor Information Centre

Town Hall Extension

Lloyd Street

St Peter's Square

Manchester M2

tel: 0161 234 3157

www.destinationmanchester.com

For details on the city's attractions; accommodation service; car hire bookings; Blue Badge walking tour bookings...

Free bus services every few minutes:

No.1: from Piccadilly Station goes via China Town; King Street; John Dalton Street; Deansgate; Marks and Spencer; Cross Street; King Street; China Town...

No.2: from Victoria Station goes via Deansgate; Peter Street; Town Hall; Princess Street; China Town; Gay Village; Whitworth Street; Oxford Road Station; Deansgate Station; Deansgate; Marks and Spencer; Selfridges;; Exchange Square; The Triangle; The Printworks; Urbis...

Metrolink operate a link between Piccadilly, the city centre, Shude Hill and Victoria; and the Eccles line goes to The Lowry (alight at Harbour City).

tel: 0161 205 2000

GMPTE Bus Station and Travel Shop in Piccadilly Gardens for No 42 services to Didsbury and Platt Hall; as well as other services to all parts of the city.

tel: 0161 228 7811

www.gmpte.com

Index